Praise fo

"Kyle Gray is an incredibly tal[...]
of spiritual seekers and [...] already converted."
GABBY BERNSTEIN, #1 *NEW YORK TIMES* BEST-SELLING AUTHOR

"Kyle Gray is an expert on celestial connections
and has the following to prove it."
YOU MAGAZINE

"I had full-bodied chills. Kyle Gray is the hottest, hippest medium who
translates the wisdom of the angels in the most loving and relatable
way possible. I couldn't recommend his brilliant spiritual gifts more."
MEGGAN WATTERSON, AUTHOR OF *MARY MAGDALENE REVEALED*

"Kyle Gray changes lives!"
THE SUN

"Kyle Gray is one of the world's most incredibly gifted angel communicators.
I have seen him work and he is authentic, intelligent, and deeply
compassionate. I highly recommend him and all his creations."
COLETTE BARON-REID, INTERNATIONAL BEST-SELLING ORACLE EXPERT

"I adore Kyle Gray. He helps you to reconnect with all that is
wanting to rise up within you, be available to the benevolent support
that already surrounds you and release what is wanting to fall
away with grace and ease. Who doesn't want some of that?!"
REBECCA CAMPBELL, AUTHOR OF *YOUR SOUL HAD A DREAM, YOUR LIFE IS IT*

"Kyle Gray... has a remarkable spiritual connection."
DAVID R. HAMILTON, PH.D., AUTHOR OF *HOW YOUR MIND CAN HEAL YOUR BODY*

"You are one tapped in light worker. I'm completely wowed by your gifts, and I'm so glad that such wisdom has come in a such hip package—you are just what the world needs right now."
DANIELLE LAPORTE, AUTHOR OF *THE DESIRE MAP*

"Kyle Gray is now one of the most successful 'angel readers' in the UK."
PSYCHOLOGIES MAGAZINE

"Kyle represents the future of spiritual wellbeing; he is both deeply insightful and wildly relatable. He gives me faith that we are in good hands for the future generations of seekers and spiritual practitioners, all while rocking a fresh pair of Jordans."
MICHAEL JAMES WONG, BEST-SELLING AUTHOR OF *SENBAZURU* AND FOUNDER OF JUST BREATHE

ANGELS ARE WITH YOU NOW

Also by Kyle Gray

Books

Raise Your Vibration
Divine Masters, Ancient Wisdom
Angel Numbers
Angel Prayers
Connecting with the Angels Made Easy
Light Warrior
Wings of Forgiveness
Angels Whisper in My Ear

Oracle Card Decks

Angelic Activations Oracle
The 22 Archangels Oracle
The Divine Masters Oracle
Raise Your Vibration Oracle
Gateway of Light Activation Oracle
The Angel Guide Oracle
Angels and Ancestors Oracle Cards
Keepers of the Light Oracle Cards

Meditations and Immersive Learning

Start Your Day with the Angels
Winding Down with the Angels
Archangel Raphael: Emerald Healing Meditation
A Day with the Angels
Angelic Assistance
and more...

ANGELS ARE WITH YOU NOW

KYLE GRAY

HAY HOUSE

Carlsbad, California • New York City
London • Sydney • New Delhi

Published in the United Kingdom by:
Hay House UK Ltd, 1st Floor, Crawford Corner, 91–93 Baker Street, London W1U 6QQ
Tel: +44 (0)20 3927 7290; www.hayhouse.co.uk

Published in the United States of America by:
Hay House LLC, PO Box 5100, Carlsbad, CA 92018-5100
Tel: (1) 760 431 7695 or (800) 654 5126; www.hayhouse.com

Published in Australia by:
Hay House Australia Publishing Pty Ltd, 18/36 Ralph St, Alexandria NSW 2015
Tel: (61) 2 9669 4299; www.hayhouse.com.au

Published in India by:
Hay House Publishers (India) Pvt Ltd, Muskaan Complex,
Plot No.3, B-2, Vasant Kunj, New Delhi 110 070
Tel: (91) 11 4176 1620; www.hayhouse.co.in

Text © Kyle Gray, 2025

The moral rights of the author have been asserted.

All rights reserved. No part of this book may be reproduced by any mechanical, photographic or electronic process, or in the form of a phonographic recording; nor may it be stored in a retrieval system, transmitted or otherwise be copied for public or private use, other than for 'fair use' as brief quotations embodied in articles and reviews, without prior written permission of the publisher.

The information given in this book should not be treated as a substitute for professional medical advice; always consult a medical practitioner. Any use of information in this book is at the reader's discretion and risk. Neither the author nor the publisher can be held responsible for any loss, claim or damage arising out of the use, or misuse, of the suggestions made, the failure to take medical advice or for any material on third-party websites.

A catalogue record for this book is available from the British Library.

Tradepaper ISBN: 978-1-4019-6857-1
E-book ISBN: 978-1-78817-807-5
Audiobook ISBN: 978-1-78817-806-8

10 9 8 7 6 5 4 3 2 1

Printed in the United States of America

This product uses responsibly sourced papers and/or recycled materials. For more information, see www.hayhouse.com.

"We rarely know, till wildered eyes
See white wings lessening up the skies,
The angels with us unawares."
GERALD MASSEY

Contents

· 1 ·

The Boy Who Sees Angels

1

· 2 ·

Do Not Be Afraid

21

· 3 ·

Who Are Angels?

37

· 4 ·

Angels Are Messengers

45

· 5 ·

Angels through the Ages

75

· 6 ·

The Spiritual Laws

93

· 7 ·

The Four Pillars

111

· 8 ·

Attracting Angels

125

· 9 ·

Speaking to Angels

145

· 10 ·

Angel Signs

171

· 11 ·

Can Humans Become Angels?

201

References 221
About the Author 223

·1·

The Boy Who Sees Angels

"We, unaccustomed to courage
exiles from delight
live coiled in shells of loneliness
until love leaves its high holy temple
and comes into our sight
to liberate us into life."

MAYA ANGELOU, "TOUCHED BY AN ANGEL"

I grew up on the west coast of Scotland about 35 minutes from Glasgow city center in Inverclyde, an area known for shipbuilding, manufacturing, and as the home of James Watt, whose enhancements to the steam engine helped usher in the Industrial Revolution. It's a beautiful part of the world, running along the River Clyde as it heads to the sea—but it's also the wettest place in Scotland!

If it wasn't for the *dreich*—miserable, cloudy, cold, and wet—weather, I imagine many of the tourists who explore the area when cruise liners dock here might one day plan to retire here for the views alone. On the few days we get sun, you'll see people strolling along the Esplanade or sitting in their cars gazing at the hills across the Firth of Clyde while enjoying our world-famous fish and chips. (You'll never find any better.) From the river to the bay, the sea, and the sky, life in Inverclyde is full of water.

I remember things from my very early childhood like the lime green color of our bathroom sink and laughing in my cot before I could speak. When I was a little older, these memories puzzled my mother. "How do you even know that?" she would ask. At the time I didn't know that I shouldn't know.

My first home was in Greenock, then when I was three and a half, we moved to a big new bungalow on a hill in Port Glasgow, three miles away. It was a redbrick square home that my parents had designed, with steps leading up to the front door and a sloping front lawn. Everything was going well. My mum was a hair stylist and my dad worked for IBM.

Ours was a street of mostly new and young families who became friends. Children would play at each other's homes and families would take turns hosting barbecues and taking the children for a swim or to the cinema. It was a lovely period of time, with the three of us and our West Highland terrier, Tora, in that bungalow in the town by the riverside.

Until one day it wasn't.

I woke one morning and couldn't get up. I'd had flu the week before, followed by some pain and tingling in my legs, but this was different. My legs wouldn't move at all. It was like a toothache feeling, numb and sore. I called my mum and my parents came into the room. My dad picked me up, and before I knew it, we were driving to the hospital. The doctors were concerned I might have meningitis.

I was moved to a specialist children's hospital. I was in and out of it for months on end, having several lumbar punctures—some of the worst experiences of my life—and all kinds of tests, until a young doctor just qualified saw my symptoms and instantly realized I had Guillain-Barré syndrome. This is a virus that attacks the immune system, shutting down part of the body and causing paralysis.

At the same time, my mother's mother, Agnes, who lived nearby, had a number of health challenges, including cancer. When I came home, my playroom was emptied of all my things and turned into a little bedroom and living area for her, and she moved in with us. Both of us were in wheelchairs.

Almost overnight, as well as working full time, my mother became a carer for two people reliant on her for almost everything. This put a lot of pressure on my parents' relationship. They begin to fight almost constantly. Loud fights. There was no escaping the sound of their anger in that bungalow on the hill.

I was quite accustomed to the wind and rain of the west coast of Scotland. But the cold from the storms in my home started to seep into my bones. However, I was beginning to learn there was a way to shelter from the storm by going inside your mind.

And there were bright spots piercing the gloom hanging over Inverclyde. Our neighbor Margaret, a devout Catholic, would come to see my nana, bringing holy water and Mother Mary trinkets that enchanted me. Sometimes she would take me to her Catholic church and help me light a candle.

Plus, Nana and I would have fun. Some days my mum would put me on Nana's lap in her wheelchair and we'd go out for hours together wrapped up in her red Royal Stewart tartan blanket. Nana carried a full kitchen blade with her everywhere. Sometimes she would take a big block of cheese and an apple out of her handbag and start slicing away and handing pieces to me that I ate happily.

Other times at home Nana tickled my back. That was my favorite thing. It gave me the sensation of really being loved. In those moments of giggling, I thought, *Maybe everything really is okay.*

But while my body healed, Nana's continued to decline. After about six months, I was able to walk again, but Nana was in and out of the hospital. Margaret began to look after me while my parents were out at the hospital in the evenings. But everyone was glad that I was able to walk again in time for my first year of primary school.

The week that school started, it was Margaret who tucked me in. I had just got a Ninja Turtles lunchbox to take to school and was so obsessed with it I wanted to take it to bed with me. Instead I had to content myself with setting it on the nightstand of my light blue room with baby-blue curtains and bedding to match.

One night, as Margaret was about to flip off the light, I asked her to please leave it on. I didn't know why.

In the middle of the night, I woke suddenly. The light had been turned off, but I could see Nana sitting on the bottom of my bed. She was obviously feeling better, because she wasn't in her wheelchair. She smelled like a combination of Olbas oil and Ralgex heat spray. I felt her love and remembered her tickling my back, and as soon as I thought of that, Nana moved toward me and started doing it. I felt so loved and supported and safe as I drifted off to sleep.

The next morning, when my mum opened the curtains, I looked around the room.

"What are you looking for, Kyle?" Mum's voice was gentle.

"Nana. Where is she? Is she in her room?"

Mum shook her head and seemed upset.

"Is she having breakfast?"

Again she shook her head.

I had a horrible thought. "She hasn't been taken back to the hospital, has she?"

Mum left the room when I asked that question.

In the kitchen, eating my cereal, I was still looking for Nana.

"Where is she, Mum? I saw her last night. She came into my room when I woke up. I'm so glad that she isn't in her wheelchair anymore. Where is she now?"

Mum couldn't find the words to tell me her mother had passed the night before. She and Dad decided to take me out for lunch and break the news then.

When I heard it, I just couldn't understand it. "How can she be in heaven? I saw her last night. She was in my room."

"That must have been a dream," my mum told me.

♦ ♦ ♦

My nana's passing opened me up at the same time as I was learning how to shut down and detach. That same week my parents' relationship came to a sudden halt when Dad moved out.

When the world didn't feel safe, I went inward. Long before I learned how to read cards or divine someone's future, I learned how to read a room. I knew how to sense if something wasn't right. Nothing escaped me, not even the faintest micro-expression passing over someone's face for the briefest moment. I was hyper-tuned. Hypersensitive. Hyper-aware.

I would go to bed at night and know I was being watched. I would feel other people in the room. Much later, I realized that somehow the ability to be a conduit between this world and the next had been switched on in me and these were spirits wanting to pass messages to people on Earth. I was experiencing a spiritual awakening, though I wouldn't have known to call it that.

It was also around this time that my migraine headaches began. I had been able to start school, but my attendance was poor due to these grueling headaches and all the medicine I had to take.

Even when I was in the classroom, I had a hard time paying attention. The teachers said I wasn't listening. I had a bunch of hearing tests in my first year of school, but my hearing was fine.

"Kyle is a dreamer," one teacher wrote on my report card.

Kyle is a dreamer.

I *was* a dreamer and I still am.

Only I *knew* that my grandmother had been sitting on my bed the night she passed, whatever other people said. I also knew that I would have to question everything from that moment onward and find my own answers.

I'd become a rebel of sorts. A freethinker.

In time, I would become an angel expert covered with tattoos, a rebellious soul staring at the opening pages of a draft of his ninth book with a black eye from a training partner's elbow at Brazilian Jiu-Jitsu.

But even way back then I knew I would have to ask the questions that would guide me toward the light. That's what I've done for the past three decades. And, despite everything I now know to be true, it's what I still do.

♦ ♦ ♦

I'm writing this book because it's the best chance I have of reaching you directly and supporting you on your spiritual journey. The answers to the questions I ask about angels change and deepen as I learn more, and that's why I keep writing books. Angels are here to help us evolve, and that means me as well.

Sometimes the learning comes through active research and contact with angels. Sometimes it's more about making space for the answers to come. In the pages ahead, we'll talk about why you needn't be afraid of an angel encounter and learn more about who angels are and how they've been represented over the years. I'll help you attract angels, welcome them in, and find ways to communicate with them, and we'll talk about recognizing and interpreting the signs they give us. Toward the end, we'll wrestle with one of the most common and poignant questions I receive: Can humans become angels?

We'll go from an abbey on an island off the coast of France that was built following a visit from Archangel Michael, to Glasgow's largest concert venue. We'll visit the apartment where I struck out on my own and the windowless office in the city center where I once gave readings, and I'll invite you into the room where I'm working today with my dogs beside me. You'll hear about some fascinating encounters with angels, from a girl who had eight of them to a psychotherapist who had a breakthrough with a patient because of a visit from an angel.

We'll start with a barbecue when I was 15. I remember it like it was yesterday. After all, it was the day that changed my life. Forever.

The Survivor

It was summer. I remember how blue the sky was, with the sun shining bright and high. It was a rarity to have a day like that in Greenock. We'd moved back there when I was about eight.

Now Mum was saying, "Come on, get your things. We don't want to keep Marion waiting."

We were on our way to a barbecue at her friend Marion's place, but I wasn't moving very fast.

"Bring your angel cards," Mum told me.

That got my attention. I grabbed my backpack and we were off.

If you've never heard of angel cards before, the best thing I can relate them to is Tarot cards. With an angel deck, however, all the cards contain a positive message, along with an image of an angel. Through intention, we can work with the cards to receive guidance and messages from angels.

Not long before, I'd got my first set of cards, and for a few months I'd been on a deep spiritual dive into the world of angels. I grew up in a loosely Christian household, though my dad didn't really follow any religion. My mother's family were Presbyterian. Her sister June married a Baptist from the Church of God and we would go to Worship Evenings at his evangelical-style church near Port Glasgow.

I also joined an interdenominational Christian youth group, Boys' Brigade. Think Christian Scouts, but with marching and Bible study. We began and ended our weekly meetings with a prayer. I liked that idea and incorporated it into my own life, starting and ending my day with a prayer as well.

I still hadn't learned much about angels, apart from how to make one out of a cardboard cone, but I had been learning about a God who wanted me to conduct myself in a certain way. This God seemed to be constantly judging me, and to be honest, I didn't like him all that much. Who wants to feel constantly judged and be told to act one specific way?

As it was, I already felt a little out of place in the world. I was a bit different from most of my peers and I always had a mixed style of interests. For example, in school the music you liked dictated the types of clothing you wore and the friends you hung out with. I loved Linkin Park and Blink-182, but I loved Beyoncé as well. I wasn't sure where I belonged.

Plus, I had always been interested in everything "unseen." I used to spook myself out reading books like the Goosebumps series. I was drawn to TV shows like *Most Haunted* and *Crossing Over with John Edward*. By the time my teenage years rolled up, a show had started on TV that would change the trajectory of my life.

On Mondays after I had read the Bible with the Boys' Brigade, I went home and watched *Buffy the Vampire Slayer*. Tarot cards, crystals, magic... Oh my goodness, I can't explain how much of an impact this show made on my life! It gave me a place to belong. Even though it was fantasy, a lot of the information in it was influenced by spiritual teachings. Soon I was researching crystals, Earth magic, ley lines, and energy healing.

I remember speaking about the show one week at Sunday school, but being dismissed by my leader, who happened to be my cousin. Eventually that cousin would give me an ultimatum, to choose between God or Buffy. And I chose... Buffy.

That was the end of the line for me and Christianity.

So, back to angel cards. In late January when I was about to turn 15, I was visiting family friends with Dad. We were in a house owned by a woman called Fiona.

Dad had bought a lottery ticket. I placed a green crystal on it and Fiona asked me why. I told her green was the color of abundance, so I was placing it on the ticket to bring good energy. Although we didn't hit the jackpot, Dad did win £10, which was 10 times his stake.

Fiona asked if I'd ever been interested in guardian angels. I shook my head and took the opportunity to tell her I'd pulled back a bit from Christian teachings, as I was tired of feeling judged.

She smiled and said, "Angels are more than a Christian idea." She told me to follow her upstairs.

Her entire room was white—white bedding, white throw, and a super fluffy bed that looked like a cloud in heaven. It was quite fitting, actually.

We sat on a corner of the bed and Fiona took some cards from a little velvet pouch and spread them across the bed.

"Hold your hands over the cards," she told me, "and when you feel warmth, pick the one you are above. You will be getting a message from your guardian angel."

I did what she had said and, oddly, I did feel warmth above a certain card, and picked it.

Turning it over, I saw *Synchronicity*. It wasn't a familiar word to me, but the card said something about how everything that occurs in life is part of a divine unfoldment. Later I looked up the word, and started hearing it and reading it quite often. It's a word that has always stayed with me.

There is a moment when you realize something is out there. The author and founder of my publishing house, Louise L. Hay, called this "a demonstration."

I had one.

Overnight I became obsessed with angels and began to read anything and everything I could about them. One of the big things that I learned was that angels could help us in our life, but as they respected our free will, they would never impose. We could, however, welcome them in.

I also read that if you meditated quietly before putting in an angelic request, you were more likely to get a response. So I decided to start sitting quietly on a routine basis and visualizing myself coated in a golden light that was coming down from the heavens. Then I would say a simple prayer: "Angels, if you're there, heal my headaches!"

My parents had tried everything. No dairy. No chocolate. No TV at night. More water. Magnesium. Medication. Everything within reach.

Doctors speculated that there was nerve damage or some sort of allergy, but we could never get to the bottom of it. Could angels help?

About four or five days after I had started this ritual, I woke up and didn't have a headache. My eyes weren't sore. I jumped out of bed, late for school as usual. I was zooming up the street when I realized everything seemed... brighter.

From that moment on, my headaches were gone. Was it a miracle? It certainly felt like that to me.

After the day I'd picked the *Synchronicity* card, I knew I had to have my own angel deck. My birthday was coming up in February and I got my own set at the bookshop with the vouchers I received as a gift. My own set of angel cards! How I treasured them. I still have that original deck in a little velvet pouch.

I began doing readings on anyone and everyone. If I went to a friend's house, I would do a reading for their mother or their aunt or their gran—anyone willing to pick some cards. Even some of the teachers at school. I made an agreement with my gym teacher that if I read her cards, I could skip the 5k runs.

I genuinely didn't know what I was doing, but I winged it. I would take the guidebook out and help people understand the card they had picked. At some point I no longer needed to look at the book—I just knew what the cards meant. Although, looking back, I was only scratching the surface of what the cards had to offer, I was starting to get positive feedback on the accuracy of my readings.

Okay, so now you know a bit about where I was on the day of the barbecue and why I was so eager to grab my deck and join my mum on the way to Marion's place.

Marion lived in an apartment block with a communal garden that had several picnic tables. Already she had a tablecloth on one of the tables and had spread out a bunch of Tupperware bowls. The barbecue was fired up.

Soon more people started to arrive, including Marion's work friend Philip, along with his partner, Jamie.

"Always fashionably late," Marion greeted the couple.

"Traffic from the city. The place was jumping!" Philip handed Marion a bottle of white Zinfandel.

Potato salad, chicken drumsticks, tuna, sweetcorn, pasta salad—you name it, it was there at that party.

As we ate, we started chatting about what we'd been up to recently. At one point Philip looked across the table and caught my eye. "What have you been up to, Kyle? Your mum says you've been interested in psychic stuff."

"I guess you could say that," I told him. "I'm really interested in guardian angels and working with cards to receive messages from them."

Philip looked somewhat surprised. He hadn't really heard about that kind of thing. I told him a little about my path toward angels and how my headaches had miraculously disappeared after I had called on them for help.

Mum broke into our conversation. "You should let him read your cards, Phil—he's getting really good. He's got so much right for all the girls at work!"

Philip said he'd give it a shot. Jamie seemed willing to try as well.

I did Philip's reading first. It turned out to be a general overview of life, but nothing that eventful. It was the reading with Jamie that activated a spiritual awakening in me.

It was clear that Jamie was a bit apprehensive as I began the reading. I spread the cards out on the table and asked him to place his hands on top of them. Then I placed mine on top of his.

I closed my eyes and said, "Just think if there's anything you would like help with." And after a moment or two, I added, "If there are any angels here now, I want to feel you. If there are any angels here now, help me give him a message."

Remember I had been trained by *Buffy*, so I was essentially summoning the spirits the way I'd learned from TV, subbing in angels for spirits and hoping it would work.

With my eyes still closed, I heard music, but not a hymn or "Ave Maria." It was "Survivor" by Destiny's Child, which had come out the year before.

"Do you hear that?" I opened my eyes.

"Hear what?"

I told him the song I was hearing. He shook his head.

I closed my eyes again and said to the angel, if there was one, "Show yourself. If there's an angel here, make your presence known."

I opened my eyes, but wasn't ready for what happened next. A light started shooting toward me from behind Jamie and suddenly there was a gigantic pillar of light on my right, his left, with big hollow black eyes. It reminded me of the film *Cocoon*. Have you seen that one?

When I looked at the angel, it didn't look at me, it looked *in* me. It was clear to me that nothing could be hidden. I can't help but shudder as I write this. I felt seen in a way I can't even describe to this day. It was as if my entire life history was on view. At the same time, in my head I could hear a really rigid voice.

"Tell this man he is a survivor."

"You are a survivor," I said to Jamie.

"Sorry?"

"You are a survivor."

"What do you mean, I am a survivor?"

In my head, I passed the message along. Suddenly the light presence started flashing images in front of my mind of Jamie trying to take his own life.

I started speaking in an almost uncontrolled voice, superfast. "You tried to leave your body. You tried to leave the Earth. But something is keeping you here. Did you try to leave your body? Did you try to kill yourself?"

Jamie stood up, adjusting his black polo shirt. "I've had enough. I've had enough. This is too much. Stop!"

The angel vanished.

"That was too much," Jamie said again. "That was too close to the bone." He whispered something to Philip and told Marion, "We're going to head up home."

And they were gone.

Mum asked me what had happened, but I knew about the code of confidentiality around readings from the angel books I'd read. "I told him what I was getting and I don't think he liked it," was all I said.

I found out later that Jamie had in fact tried to take his own life on multiple occasions, but each time something had stopped him. Once he'd hanged himself and woken up separate from the noose.

Later Mum heard the story from Marion, who'd heard it from Jamie. Word spread over the telephone lines. The very next day, people started calling and asking Mum, "Is your son the boy who can see angels? I'd like to speak to him."

·2·

Do Not Be Afraid

"If you knew who walked beside you at all times, on the
path that you have chosen, fear would be impossible."

A COURSE IN MIRACLES

That first angel encounter was quite heavy and ended with Jamie asking me to stop, but as you'll realize by now, it didn't exactly put me off spiritual exploration. I admit, though, I was always a little bit scared of the dark. A bit spooked by the unseen.

It's hard not to be scared when it comes to spiritual stuff, because the media has always portrayed it as frightening. If you've seen the famous angel scene in the film *Angels in America*, you'll know it's hardly a subtle sequence when Prior, the protagonist, has an encounter with an angel. And if you haven't seen the film (you should), it starts with the entire room vibrating, the lampshade bursting into flames, and the bed starting to shake and almost levitate. Prior hangs on to it like he's on a surfboard on top of an uncontrollable wave. Finally, the roof is ripped off and falls all around him. He looks up, covered in dust, to see an angel with giant widespread wings coming down, proclaiming, "The messenger has arrived."

I don't know about you, but that would freak me out! And this kind of portrayal is common throughout all kinds of books and films, with characters shown as victims of circumstance rather than creators of their own narrative. Many of us have learned that if we come into contact with a being from outside our material world, we'll be victims as well.

And there's more. Many religions teach that psychic experiences, including speaking to spirits, are demonic. Although in Catholicism the "Guardian Angel Prayer" is a favorite of many, Baptists will tell you not to speak directly to your angel. Those of us who grew up in more traditional religious spaces often heard, "You shouldn't be meddling with anything unseen! That's a sin. That's devil worship. Satanic!"

Okay—that's a little creepy. No wonder we're a little bit afraid. The patriarchy wants to keep us feeling powerless, and this dynamic is reinforced through the kind of imagery that depicts encounters with the unseen as traumatic, overwhelming, and out of our control. All kinds of people stand to gain a lot by keeping us in the dark about our own power. We're easier to repress and govern when we're scared and feel we can't make decisions about our own lives. When we become our own seers, on the other hand, we're tasked with taking the lead in our own life. (For some, that's *really* scary!)

So, with all these frightening portrayals and devil-worship warnings, why aren't more people saying that it can feel scary to think about seeing an angel? I've started to think a big reason is because fear is seen as weak. It can still be present, of course. But at one time I used to wonder, *Am I the only one who's scared? Does anyone else feel this way?*

When I was 15 or 16, I asked one of the mediums at the Spiritualist church about it. Spiritualism is a religious movement that is based on the belief that those in the spirit world can communicate with the living. When Mum saw a Spiritualist meeting advertised in the paper, we'd decided to go along. The medium was the same woman as before, and yet again she gave accurate names, dates, places, and addresses, and described the person she was communicating with on the other side in great detail. There and then, I told Mum that was exactly what I was put on this Earth to do.

I did deliver messages in the Spiritualist church later on and it helped me learn how to address an audience and how to pray openly too.

I would often ride share to the meetings with a medium called Tillie (short for "Matilda"). It started with her driving me, but when I got my license and could borrow a car from my mum or dad, I'd pick her up. She was a feisty woman in her late eighties. When she laughed, her false teeth would bump off one another. She would often come to the meetings with a walker, but when she was demonstrating hands-on spiritual healing or channeling a message to the congregation, she didn't need any support. It was almost as if unseen angels were giving her the strength to step into the role of service and hope that she loved so much.

One night in late summer, we went in early to help set up the tea and coffee for the congregants and I asked her if she'd ever felt scared of seeing spiritual beings.

"*Nope!*" she said with a cheeky smile. "It's the living that I'm more scared of."

I believed Tillie, but I didn't feel that what she said necessarily applied to me. All I could do was tell myself that maybe one day I'd overcome this hesitation.

I think there's a lot we can learn by looking directly into this fear. I mean, we're talking about something pretty powerful here. We're not contemplating something as commonplace as feeling terrified when preparing to speak in front of an audience. I've given talks in front of audiences of 5,000, and even though the Leo Ascendant in my astrological chart says I was born for the limelight, I'm still nervous every time I step on stage.

It was actually on stage, at the World Angel Congress in Hamburg, Germany, fairly recently, that I admitted that when I read about angels late at night, I used to be worried one was going to appear.

And then I asked the question I usually just come right out with now: "Who here is scared of seeing an angel?"

Usually no one puts up a hand. Next, I ask, "Who has read a book about angels and in the back of their mind had the thought, *I would love to know you're there, but at the same time don't come out right now?*"

The whole audience shoot their hands up and roar with laughter.

Through these kinds of open conversations, I've begun meeting many others who thought the idea of having an encounter with a phenomenal cloaked being was fascinating, but a little bit frightening as well.

Okay, so it wasn't just me! Well, that's a relief.

If it's you, here's where I want to tell you something I've learned in the two decades since those meetings with Tillie that I hope will be comforting. It has to do with free will. Angels—and the entire spiritual realm—only act in accordance with your free will. That's how powerful you already are.

So, angels won't come into your life unless you give them permission. In fact, if any kind of energy comes into your space and you don't want it there, you can decide not to welcome it.

♦ ♦ ♦

This is a good time to tell you about Mary, the mother of Christ. If you've read some of my other books, you'll know how much I adore her. Or if you've been to my upstairs bathroom. (It's full of Mary statues.) Whether you believe in Scripture or not, I think that Mary's story can help us think about fear in the context of a spiritual experience.

Probably the first time I heard about Mary was when Margaret brought the Miraculous Medals of Mary to my grandmother's bedside. Since then, through all the dark times in my life, just like in The Beatles' song, Mary has been there.

So, let's put ourselves back in the ancient world, in a small village called Nazareth not far from the Sea of Galilee, under the rule of the Roman Empire. The village is isolated, surrounded by hills, and not on any significant trade routes. All the main action is happening down in Jerusalem.

A young Jewish girl is living a quiet life there with her family. She is betrothed to a man named Joseph. And one day she gets a visit from Archangel Gabriel, who tells her she will be the mother of Jesus, who will be the son of God. Quite a message for a devout Jewish girl.

——————————— ◆ ———————————

Archangels are like CEO angels; they
govern all the guardian angels.

————————————————————————

By the way, most likely Gabriel was Gabrielle, or appeared feminine, if anything. There's speculation that all the feminine descriptions of angels were at one point changed to masculine to support the patriarchal system. Whenever I get the chance, I lobby for feminine spiritual voices to rise. Call me a feminist, if you like. Oh, and one more thing on the topic of films—Gabrielle is perfectly portrayed by Tilda Swinton in the film *Constantine*! Now, back to the story.

The first thing Gabrielle says is, "Do not be afraid."

That line has always haunted me. Maybe because for so long I *was* afraid.

Gabrielle gives Mary a reason not to be afraid. She says, "For I am an angel of the lord."

That's super important, so let's pause for a minute. I mean, something quite incredible is going on here, right?

I spent a long time just sitting with Gabrielle's words. I read everything I could about Mary. I devoured *Alone of All Her Sex: The myth and the cult of the Virgin Mary*, a massive book by Marina Warner.[1] This helps us understand why Mary has assumed such a goddess-type role in the world and how what she represents is probably what the world needs now more than ever.

I remember one night I had spiritual books spread out all around me on the bed and I was just playing that line over and over in my head: *Do not be afraid. Do not be afraid.*

I wondered why it felt so haunting. Perhaps because that's where the idea of free will came from?

Why? Gabrielle is described as "burning with fire." Remember we're a few thousand years back, when there were no artificial light sources. The only light source was fire, including the sun. So, that young girl must have been experiencing an overwhelming mix of feelings when that being appeared. Fear, for sure, at first, I would think. Maybe she was wondering if what she was seeing was real.

The angel takes the time to acknowledge this. But is she telling Mary not to be afraid because she's human and she's having an encounter with a supernatural being? Or is there another layer here, because at that time only rabbis and prophets were allowed to have angelic encounters—that is, only men with great power? Mary was a normal Jewish girl in an unremarkable agricultural village. She wasn't even the daughter of a rabbi. Yet she was receiving a visitation. Was that the reason why she might be afraid?

Or was it something else? It's pretty powerful to have an angel come down and greet you, right? It was powerful for Mary, and it's powerful for us as well. It's unnerving maybe at first to think of our guardian angel always watching over us. We're used to privacy, at least offline.

And here's the scariest part, maybe; it's the thread that runs through this whole book: If we accept an angel's guidance—if we invite angelic guidance into our life—we're accepting a power that comes with a certain amount of responsibility. There is a life of devotion and deeper meaning available to us—so much more than we can measure or capture through data analytics or on the camera on our iPhone. It's awesome in the true sense of the word. But it means accepting there's a purpose for our life and doing our best to fulfil that.

For that young girl in Galilee, that meant becoming the mother of Christ. And if you're into that kinda thing, it's a big deal! For many, he became the king of kings.

This thought about free will came to me on stage. I was at the Angel Congress in Salzburg. All the hours spent reading and wondering and contemplating Gabrielle's words came together in one "Aha!" moment as I was speaking to an audience. *Mary doesn't have to agree.*

Mary has a choice. As we know, of course, she accepts the offer, saying, "Let all of what you say be true."

And there's a lesson here for all of us. We also have a choice when we have an encounter with an angelic being. We can decide whether we want to say "yes" or "no" to what that entails. So, in short, Mary's angelic encounter is a story of choice.

◆ ◆ ◆

So, yes, it is a bit scary to know that once you welcome angels in, your life can never be the same again. I can't lie to you about that. And change *is* scary. So is responsibility. It's easier to be a follower than a leader.

It's not easy to be different either. "Who is this guy who thinks he can speak to angels? He's delusional."

It got to the point where, when I was around 20, I gave up on "doing angels." I think one of the toxic traits in my life is that I want to be liked, and I didn't really want to be the oddball anymore.

In fact, being "the angel guy" had been draining for a lot of different reasons. Everyone wanted a piece of me. "Read my aura. Read my palm. Tell me something. Prove yourself."

So I took a day job as an events director in a Glasgow hotel and on weekends I started to DJ. That took off very quickly—a guy at a club I loved hired me right away, I won a famous Scottish festival's superstar DJ competition, and I was signed by an agency and soon had a calendar full of gigs where I could lead the party and be cool.

That's what music gave me.

But angels were never far away.

One night after I got home from DJing, I started reading a Diana Cooper book. I turned to Chapter 5, "Feathers," and a little feather fell out of the book, a light came into the room, and I felt loved. I fell asleep in the love, and the next morning when I woke up, there beside my bed was a gigantic Black angel, wearing armor.

Why are you here? I was thinking. Did I even want to see whoever this was? What about being the cool kid?

I think the angels were asking me, "Do you want us to be a bigger part of your life or not? Do you want to follow this spiritual path, or not?"

That was the day I said "yes" to the angels.

◆ ◆ ◆

Later that same day the *Scottish Sun* newspaper called me up, looking for a columnist. So I set out on the path that would take me across the world and eventually to this page. This path keeps taking me outward, to the stage, through international publishing deals, and onto the *Wall Street Journal* bestseller list. But going inward is the center of the experience. If you can go inward, you can have everything you think I have, or at least everything that matters. And you don't need me in order to have it. My prayers aren't any louder than yours. Angels are with you now.

Isn't that just kind of incredible to contemplate? Even better, angels are approachable. They're joyful. They're fun. They're the kind of energy you want to be around.

When we acknowledge the angels around us, when we let love in, despite the fear, we're inviting light. We're learning how to *become* light. And eventually there's so much light and love, there's no room for fear.

———————————— ♦ ————————————

Wherever love is present, fear is a stranger.
The next time you're scared, think about those you love.

————————————————————

A lot of us are so scared of being scared that we stop ourselves from having an experience that would bring us peace and happiness. We resist entering a sanctuary that's available to us at any hour, in any space.

That sanctuary, that inner landscape, is a place of introspection, patience, practice, quiet. It is not the loud space of optimization, reaching outward, and continually setting new goals. I am not critical of goal-setting—I do it myself quite often and it's largely how I've managed my career. It can be a fruitful approach and I've seen this among my friends and in my circles. But I am critical of not giving yourself time to explore. As you'll see in the chapters ahead, I like to stay in the inquiry of it all. To me, this is the most generative space.

What do you think?

You don't have to answer that right away. Take some time to sit with these thoughts. Maybe you see things differently. I welcome your experience. This is my version of a life lived with angels. I'm not more special than you. That's one of the essential messages I want to get across here. Okay, I've shown over two decades that I can connect to angels and I've helped a lot of people by opening up a channel to their angels and their departed loved ones. But what I want you to take away isn't that angels are with *me*. It's that they're with *you*.

Yes, *you*. What I have is also yours to have. I don't have special access. We all come from the same source, both the most powerful among us and the least. No one is holier than anyone else. Love has forgotten no one.

I think some of us have actually had encounters with angels, but we haven't recognized them for what they were. Maybe we've put a different narrative on the experience, like the way my parents told me my grandmother sitting on the end of my bed was a dream.

As we've seen, we may be afraid because of things we've learned about angels from films, books, family, teachers, or even pastors. But having responsibility is scary all on its own. Free will isn't for the faint of heart. As Elizabeth J. Andrew tells us in her book *Writing the Sacred Journey*, "We fear our creative power. We shudder at the potential influence of our own voices."[2]

You do have a choice. You can live passively, or actively. You can let others dictate your life's course, or you can decide to raise your vibration and get in there and start making things happen. Angels will be with you no matter what you decide, not even a heartbeat away.

If you want to be in touch with them, then I invite you to enter a quieter realm. Feelings emerge when we give them time, and for me, feelings are at the heart of angel relationships, as they're at the heart of any relationship.

I've had revelations on stage in front of thousands and I've had moments that brought me to tears alone in my bedroom, storm howling outside. But I do think all the quiet I've invited into my life is what has put me on the right path to receive onstage revelations and to make many of the meaningful connections in my life.

"Do not be afraid to be alone" is what I am saying.

Because you're not.

I hope the guidance I provide and the questions I consider in this book will help you develop a closer relationship with angels, but you should know from the start that they've always been beside you.

♦ ♦ ♦

When I started writing this book, I came upon a box of notes from the time when I was a columnist for the *Scottish Sun*. It was quite weird looking at what people had written, but a lot of the messages were really uplifting. One woman wrote, "I feel a sense of happiness I've not felt for a long time. And it's thanks to you, Kyle."

Mostly people told me they felt super positive after the readings. But some were disappointed. One of the letters was from a man called Alistair. In our session, we had been able to make contact with his wife, who had passed away some years before, and this was a very profound experience for him, naturally. He expressed his deep gratitude for the chance to connect with his darling wife. But he still couldn't get over her death, he told me in the letter. He would "visualize her by [his] side and feel her love." Even with the comfort of that image and that feeling, he wrote, "the days are long, and the nights are dark."

The days are long, and the nights are dark.

Mary the mother of Christ certainly had her share of long days and dark nights, as do we all.

As I am writing in the northern hemisphere, the days are getting longer. And I don't have a remedy for the pain of the human experience. Even angels can't give us that. And yet pain is what brought me to angels. We will all face periods in our lives when the days are long, and the nights are dark. All I can say is I am grateful we don't have to face them alone.

·3·

Who Are Angels?

"Everyone who has had an angelic encounter has
seen something different from everyone else
who has seen or experienced an angel."

EILEEN ELIAS FREEMAN

So, who are these beings who accompany us through all the ups and downs of life?

The first time I heard about angels was during the lead-up to Christmas in my first year of school. I had been selected to be one of the three wise men in the nativity play. A blonde-haired girl played the angel Gabriel. She was so cute in a white frock outlined with sparkly ribbon and a halo made of tinsel streaming behind her hairband.

That December in class we all made an angel for the top of our Christmas tree. The teacher gave us each a cardboard cone for the angel's head and body and encouraged us to cut wings out of paper, decorate them with glitter and paint, and stick them onto the body.

At home, after we'd hung up the rest of the decorations, my parents lifted me up to place my angel at the top of our tree.

"Who are angels?" I asked them, pleased with how my angel looked perched on top of the green branch.

But their responses were vague. I remember being told something like, "The angel at the top of the tree will watch over us, and your presents too!"

Hmmm, that didn't tell me a whole lot.

♦ ♦ ♦

Did you learn about angels as a child? Do you have any early memories of hearing about them? Playing one in a pageant? What have you learned in the years since then? Do angels feel approachable to you? Do they feel real?

If you come from a religious background, you might have some idea about what angels are and what they can do, but the subject may still be shrouded in mystery. That's where people like me come in—I want to change that.

The word "angel" comes from the Greek word ἄγγελος, *angelos*, which means "messenger of God." (*We'll talk more about their messenger role in the following chapter.*) It's used across the world to describe an unseen being that is dedicated to guiding, healing, and protecting a person, country, or even the world. It's Abrahamic in origin, meaning it is used in all the world religions that stem from the teachings of Abraham. These include Judaism, Islam, and Christianity, but angels themselves are not bound by religion or tradition. In fact, I believe their presence predates human religion entirely.

No matter how much or little we've learned about angels in our lives, most of us know that they're positive. If someone's been helpful to us, we might say, "You're an angel," or we might even describe a peaceful sleeping baby as an angel.

♦

When you call someone "an angel,"
you invite their angelic qualities out.

Most people do believe in angels, in the United States at least. In fact, the polls around this subject are amazing! A 2023 poll conducted by NORC at the University of Chicago revealed that seven in ten Americans believed in angels (69 per cent).[1,2] Another poll showed that 36 per cent believed they'd either had an encounter with or been helped by an angel.[3] And what's cooler is that four out of every ten who believe don't follow a particular religion or tradition. In the UK, one in every three people believe in angels, according to a poll conducted by the Bible Society.[4]

Most people also think of angels as winged beings that float down from above, bursting with light, like the character that John Travolta played in the film *Michael*, but those representations are limited. Angels are so much more than that.

You can also have your very own personal experience with them, and I'm here to encourage you to trust in your own personal experience. This reminds me of Anita Moorjani's fantastic memoir about how she became cancer-free after almost dying from Hodgkin's lymphoma. It's called *Dying to be Me: My journey from cancer, to near death, to true healing*.[5] Anita's message is that we have to trust in our own self-worth and our intuition. "Following a personal spiritual path, however," she writes, "means to follow the promptings of our own inner being and taps into the infinite self we all are at our core."[6] For Anita, leaning into her own ability to trust herself meant releasing expectations and ushering in new possibilities for healing and peace.

I believe Anita is right that the center of our healing journey will be our own personal experiences. My goal is to teach you what I know and support you as you follow your own path and learn from what your inner "infinite self" already knows.

―――――――――――― ♦ ――――――――――――

Angels can appear in many forms, shapes, and sizes.

―――――――――――――――――――――――――

Your experience of angels will be unique, and one reason for this is that angels are pure energy and can appear to us in various forms, depending on our thoughts. As you know, I've seen a gigantic pillar of light with big hollow black eyes and a Black man dressed as a warrior. I've also seen a stunning woman in a long gown with golden hair flowing over her shoulders. Sometimes I get a detailed picture right down to eye color, and sometimes it's more like a beam of light.

I used to describe angels as individual beings, but I have come to learn they're part of the One, part of the whole. If the Universe or God were a heart, every time that heart beats, the beat would be an angel. When I'm in touch with an angel, I'm in touch with the heart of God. There is no separation between them.

So, angel experiences are divine and can be incredibly varied. Sometimes there are multiple angels to behold. Which leads me to one of my favorite angel stories.

The Girl with Eight Angels

When I was a columnist at the *Scottish Sun*, I once made an appearance at a meet-and-greet in Glasgow's George Square, along with other columnists. We were inside a gigantic gala tent, and there were close to 4,000 people there. I was sharing a stand with Joan Charles, who was the newspaper's resident Psychic Joan. I was speaking about guardian angels and Joan was doing handbag readings. This unusual form of psychic reading would tell people about their personality and life by the shape, type, and color of their bag and its contents. People loved it and it was very entertaining!

At one point audience members were invited to approach us to ask questions and book private sessions. I looked up to see a woman coming toward me with a skinny little blonde girl who was maybe 11 or 12. They were waving at me and I could see angels walking with the girl.

She's got so many angels! I marveled as I waved back.

When they came up to me, the woman said, "My daughter's been really desperate to meet you."

"That's so nice," I said, smiling at the girl.

Then the girl asked, "Can you see anything?"

"Funny you should ask," I told her. "As you were walking up, I could see eight angels with you."

"How many?"

"Eight. You've got eight guardian angels with you."

The mother jumped in. "Well, my daughter's died eight times."

"Yeah, look," said the girl, showing me a big, gruesome scar on her chest.

Apparently she'd had several open-heart surgeries and each time she'd felt that she'd been saved by an angel. She'd even seen an angel bringing her back to her body and had the sensation of speaking directly to God.

She'd been searching for a while for someone to validate her experience and it turned out to be me.

This little girl knew what I want you to know—we are surrounded by beings who can help us in our lives. We took a photo together and I smiled as I watched the girl walk away with a skip in her step.

My editor heard about this meeting and called me. "How the fuck did you do it, you spooky bastard?" he said, then hung up the phone.

Soon after, the *Sun* ran the story:

> *"The little girl with eight angels."*

It was really quite amazing.

♦ ♦ ♦

Who are angels? I've begun to answer the question in this chapter. But only just begun. The answers are infinite, and you will also provide your own.

In the past two decades, I've been blessed to be a vessel for divine messages from angels. Because one of those infinite answers is that angels are messengers.

· 4 ·

Angels Are Messengers

"Good news from heaven the angels bring,
Glad tidings to the earth they sing:
'To us this day a child is given,
To crown us with the joy of heaven.'"

MARTIN LUTHER

After my parents split and my mum started working around the clock, I spent most afternoons after school playing in the street with the neighboring kids. I remember my mum used to send me with a plastic bag packed with a tin of soup to Margaret's for my lunch. On weekends I would visit my dad, who had moved into an apartment with flatmates. I thought his new place was so cool. I remember each room had its own individual lock.

Once, when I was 10, Susan, one of the ladies on our street, wanted to have a psychic party. She needed six people willing to have a reading for £20 so she could get a famous psychic called Gladys to her house. My mum said she wouldn't mind taking a spot, but she would be out doing hair until late that evening, so they gave her the last slot.

When Gladys arrived, she had something else in mind, saying there was someone missing that she needed to talk to. Susan told her they were just waiting on one other person. Gladys said she knew that, and she didn't want to be told her name, as she knew exactly who she was, and she couldn't get rid of the spirits looking for this particular woman, so needed to speak to her first.

Susan had no choice but to call my mum up. Mum was giving a customer a perm and she couldn't very well leave in the middle! But in the end she did cut out of her appointment and ran down the street to Susan's house.

"You're Diane?" Gladys didn't bother with a hello.

Mum nodded. When she had caught her breath, she explained that she didn't really believe in this kind of thing.

"Why are you here then?" Gladys asked.

Mum shrugged, unfazed by Gladys' curt manner. "Curiosity," she said.

"Curiosity killed the cat," Gladys retorted. "Well, will you hurry up and sit down because your mum wants to speak to you!"

Stunned, Mum sat down.

"There's a man who wants to speak to you as well," Gladys told her. "His name is Hughey."

Mum paid attention. "I knew a Hughey."

"I can see you in a bridesmaid's dress and Hughey is there as well."

"I was his daughter's bridesmaid," Mum said.

"He's here to thank you. Did you help save his life once?" Gladys asked.

Flashback: One Friday night my mum had been walking home when she'd found her next-door neighbor Hugh Woods, nicknamed Hughey, lying on the side of the road. With the help of passers-by, she'd been able to revive him. Turned out he'd had a heart attack.

Now, before Mum could even process what was happening, Gladys was saying, "Diane, Diane, Diane," in exactly the cadence and tone of my nana in the final stages of her life.

"Who's Agnes?"

"That's my mum." Mum was a bit choked with emotion at this point.

"She can see you standing looking in the mirror, wearing the black mini-skirt."

Mum was recently divorced and had lost a lot of weight. She was the slimmest she'd been since her teens and had just bought a black mini-skirt for a night out with her girlfriends.

"She wants to speak to her blue-eyed boy."

This was one of the things my nana had always called me.

Gladys looked directly into my mother's eyes. "He saw her after she'd passed. He's going to do the same work as me. By the time he's seventeen years old, his name will be in the newspaper. He'll be known around the country for doing this work. He'll be traveling the world with it, and you'll never question what he can see and what he can hear, because it will be beyond anything you've ever imagined."

Wild, right?

Before I even get to discussing this prophecy, I want to pause to discuss the fact that Gladys had confirmed that I had seen my grandmother the night she passed. I hadn't been going nuts or hallucinating or dreaming. In a way, she played the same role here as I did when I met the girl with eight angels. As a young boy, I had in fact had an encounter with life after death—the first of many.

And then there was the third part of Gladys' message... Something big was going to happen to me.

♦ ♦ ♦

Years later, after I'd started reading cards and having some initial success, I was interviewed by the *Daily Mail* and then Mum and I headed to the Mediterranean for a holiday. She'd found a cruise deal on a Friday and we set sail the following Monday. When we arrived back in the UK after a week of eating, sleeping, and exploring the ports of Tunisia, Pisa, Nice, and Menorca, there was my name in the newspaper:

> *"'I can see angels': The* Daily Mail *meets the youngest medium in the UK"*

It was exactly as Gladys had predicted so many years before. I did become a medium, for sure, and was well known by the time I was just 17, but there's a word I have come to prefer to "medium" or "psychic." It's "messenger."

I identify as a messenger. Seems that's always been my role in life. Even back in my first school reports the teacher noted how enthusiastically I joined in class discussions. These days with my friends and various communities, I organize, I rally, I take the lead. I'm the instigator of get-togethers, the setter-up of chat conversations. Whenever there's an author trip, I immediately set up a group chat. I arrange for us all to meet up in the lobby for a coffee or in the bar the first night for a *Cheers*. If I'm going for a walk in the morning with one friend, I'll send out a message to everyone else: "Anyone want to join us?" Sometimes the friend will tell me, "I would have preferred it was just us," but for me, the more, the merrier! I've set up a group for my neighborhood as well.

I think that connecting people is what I'm meant to do. I'm meant to communicate with angels and read cards, but I'm meant to connect people as well. I really don't like the feeling of anyone being left out. I know what that feels like. I want people to know they've always got company. That's the central message of my work.

I once met a woman named Tina who had had an incredible angelic encounter. Our lives intersected 10 years ago, when I received a phone call from a TV company who wanted to shoot a pilot in Florida for a series about real-life angel encounters. Tina's had happened a few years earlier.

Tina and Damian were a young couple celebrating their anniversary. They had a newborn baby at home, staying with a babysitter for the night. The two hardly ever went out for a date night and were both excited to try a fancy restaurant not too far from their home. They enjoyed a beautiful anniversary dinner, but on the way home, a man who was driving down the other side of the highway crossed the barrier. Just before the impact, Damian had turned the car to try to avoid the crash, but the incoming car hit them head on at close to 70 mph on the side where Tina was sitting.

At this point Damian blacked out, and he woke up to find he was on fire, along with the entire car. Cars had stopped behind him and Good Samaritans from those cars were tugging at his car doors. They managed to free him, pulling him onto the road and patting him down to put out the fire.

At the same time, Tina realized the car was on fire and she was going to die. In what she thought were her final moments, she prayed, "Dear God, I've heard there's a special place in heaven for those who ask for forgiveness. Please forgive me for all my sins."

At that moment, she saw an angel put its hands on the window. Next, somehow the angel had scooped her up and was taking her upward.

At the same time, onlookers were watching a man all in black running from the side of the highway into the fire, ripping open Tina's door, pulling her out, and placing her on the ground at the side of the highway near her husband.

When Tina regained consciousness, she could hear Damian screaming. He had third-degree burns over much of his body. She looked up into a stranger's face. The man in black. He was holding her face, saying, "You're going to be okay."

Help arrived, and while Tina was being placed in the ambulance, she heard people around her saying, "Did you see the angel?"

By this time the man had disappeared.

Damian and Tina felt they'd been given another chance and wanted to give something back, so when they had recovered, they decided to adopt a little girl into their family. Damian went on to write a book about their experience as well.

When we met, it was obvious they weren't comfortable with the idea of channeling or mediumship, based on their Christian faith. However, I was able to relate to their understanding of the world because of the Christianity I'd been exposed to in childhood.

I asked Tina if she'd ever had any other encounters with angels. She told me that she'd seen them throughout her life. On one occasion, she'd been at church, singing along to songs of praise and thanking God for the fact that she'd been saved by an angel, when angels had appeared in the form of golden light coming down from the ceiling and swirling around the congregants. One had even passed close by her.

"When you saw those angels," I said, "did you ask them what their message was?"

She said she hadn't, and so of course I asked her why not. Her reason was simple: "I didn't realize that was an option."

Like many Christians, Tina had learned that you shouldn't communicate with angels directly. She'd always felt angels had messages for her family, but she didn't know how to get them.

I told her what I believed: "You could have just spoken to the angels. They were right there."

That night as I was going to bed at the motel, I started to go into a dream state during my prayers and meditation. In my head I said, "If the angel of this couple is here, thank you for revealing any message you have for them."

What came through was a voice saying clearly, "We want Damian to know it wasn't his fault."

The next day, when I passed this message on to Damian, he started to cry. Tina instantly grabbed his hand and began to cry as well.

"You have always felt the whole crash was your fault," I explained, "but the angels want you to know that God has forgiven you. You just need to forgive yourself."

"If I hadn't turned the car, it wouldn't have hit you head on," Damian said through his tears to Tina.

She told him she didn't blame him for anything and they hugged.

It was a profound moment, but very few people ever got to see it, and no one was able to watch the series, because the pilot never came to anything. Still, it was an honor to have the opportunity to receive and pass along this message for the couple. I hope they now know they can ask angels directly for a message. Many people don't realize that when they're having these encounters, they can contribute to them.

This goes for you, too. You can participate in the meaning that unfolds from an angel encounter. Let the angels know you're open to this by saying, "I can see you. I can feel you. I'm grateful for your presence and any message you want to share."

♦ ♦ ♦

I've had some pretty dramatic experiences as a messenger. I remember another where the message that came through was about forgiveness, but in a very different form.

One sunny summer Saturday I headed into the city and got to the door of my office at about 11:30. As I was getting out my key, a woman with blond hair approached me, followed by a tall boy and a girl who was maybe a year younger.

"Hiya," I said. "Waiting to see me?"

She said she was.

"Are you coming in at twelve?" I asked.

"Yes," she said.

"Do you mind coming back then?" I was saying when she grabbed my arm.

"I need to speak to you now," she said. "I don't know how long I've got."

She looked round the hall and I instantly knew there was going to be something dark involved—and that was before I'd even tuned in!

I managed to get inside my office for just two minutes before she followed me in, but it was enough time to thank Archangel Michael for putting me in the light of his protection.

Feeling that peace, I welcomed the woman in. The kids went to wait in Caffè Nero downstairs.

"I want to say something to you before we start," she said. "I do not want to know if there are any dead people here." She was a bit breathless, but kept going. "If you can see any dead people around me, I don't want to know about it. I'm happy with angels, but I don't want to hear from the dead."

I explained a bit about my process, found out her name was Sheena, and got her to put her hands over the angel cards that I'd spread out on the table. I put my hands over hers and told her to think about any area where she would like some help. I also said a little prayer: "Angels, thank you for revealing their life to me."

Instantly I saw a fight in my head—a man and woman punching, pushing, kicking, and screaming. All of a sudden, I felt a thrust to my stomach and I actually made a noise out loud as if I'd been punched. Then I looked at my hands and they were covered in blood.

"Someone's been murdered," I said.

"I wouldn't call it murder," Sheena said slowly.

"I'll tell you what's happening right now," I said. "There's blood on my hands and I'm reading you. If there's blood on my hands, there's blood on your hands. Have you killed someone?"

"Yes."

That's how the reading started.

"I see two angels in my head," I continued. "They're bringing a really tall man here. He's got his hands behind his back and an angel on either side of him. It's almost like he's being transferred to or from prison. He's saying, 'Tell her I forgive her.'"

Sheena pulled her hands away from mine. "Get that fucking low-life out of here now!" she hissed.

"He's here and he wants you to forgive him," I said calmly, knowing my job was simply to pass the message along.

"Get him fucking out!" Sheena yelled.

I felt the situation was getting beyond my level of expertise. Still, I knew I was getting the message for a reason.

"It feels as if this man is your partner of sorts—is that correct?" I asked.

"Yes," said Sheena.

"Did you kill him?"

"Yes."

"You had a fight, and he was abusive."

She nodded.

I came to learn that she had killed her boyfriend to stop him attacking her son. She'd intervened with a knife, and while it would have been classified as self-defense or manslaughter if she'd called 999 straightaway, what she had done instead meant it was classified as murder.

"Why does he want me to speak about your son?" I asked.

Sheena put her face in her hands. "He helped hide the body."

At that point I asked the angels to hold any further messages until I'd calmed the energy of the room down. What was I supposed to do, even from a legal perspective?

"You're putting me in a bit of a difficult place," I said. "What exactly is it you want from me?"

"I've been caught by the police," she said, "and they've recovered the body. I'm currently out on bail, but I know I'll be going to prison and I want to know if my son will be okay. And... am I going to hell at the end of this?"

I asked the angels and relayed the message back. Her son would be going to prison as well. He would be classified and tried as an adult for helping to hide the body, even though he was only 15.

As for Sheena's second question, I wasn't sure I believed in hell, but I told her I would ask the question.

The angels had an answer immediately: "She's already in hell. It only exists in the mind."

"Ah, I see," I said. "The reason your ex-partner wants you to forgive him is so that you can be free of the pain he caused you and free of the hell of suffering and resentment in your mind."

I ended the reading there, because I felt it wasn't right for me to continue in such hostile energy, but a few weeks later I saw Sheena again: on the front cover of the newspaper, being tried for murder. Inside the same paper was my column on angels. Even as she headed into a life behind bars, I hoped she would be able to free herself from her burden of pain.

◆ ◆ ◆

As I think these stories have demonstrated, angel experiences can be quite dramatic, but they can be subtle as well. The subtle ones can be just as important as we walk along our spiritual path. So, let's open our minds to all kinds of angel encounters, including the simplest ones you can possibly imagine.

Simplicity

When people think of meditation, many picture someone sitting on an empty beach or in a Zen garden, perfectly still and quiet, but we can meditate sitting on our couch or a park bench, or if you're like me, on our bed. If you have a yoga mat and can roll it out and light a candle, great. But you don't have to have any specific set-up to reap the benefits.

We can take this idea and apply it to angels. If we're set on how an angel will look or act, we might miss an angel experience happening right in front of us.

What do you think angels look like? How do you imagine they sound? Or act?

What if you're sitting in bed at night and a gentle calmness comes over you. Could that be a message from an angel?

What if you're struggling with a problem at work and you instantly get a solution? Could that be a message from an angel? Why not?

Or maybe you're in the middle of an argument with someone you love, and even though you know you're right, something in you says, "Make it okay. Let it go. Be gentle." Maybe that's an angel.

Angel messages can be a lot simpler than we think.

Angels hover round us. They communicate. They bring tidings. They help us grow. They are with us at threshold moments, at crucial life transitions. And at other times too. In their myriad shapes and forms, they are always there to give us support. The question is: are we listening?

◆ ◆ ◆

Just as I started working on this book, my cat Ralph passed away. Ralph was named after Archangel Raphael, whose name means "God heals," and he brought healing into my life during his years here with me. But last February, three strange things happened right in a row that told us he was unwell. My mum had bought me cakes which were delivered for Valentine's Day. I came downstairs and Ralph had thrown the box on the floor, broken it open, and eaten all the buttermilk frosting off. That was weird. And then the next day he was running around the lounge with the dogs, which was out of character for him. The following night he slept downstairs instead of in his usual spot in the guest room upstairs with Mum, who was living with me at the time. Three odd things.

That night Mum said, "I think Ralph's gonna die."

I went directly into healer mode. "We just have to monitor him," I told her.

The vet wanted me to drive into the city with Ralph, but I could feel that he wasn't going to make the trip. Instead, I put him on the bedroom floor, and I got still with him. When he started struggling a little bit, I put my hand on him and said, "Thank you, angels, for taking him into the light." In less than a minute, he stopped breathing.

I know the angels carried him swiftly away. I thanked them once again, opened myself to any messages they wanted me to receive, and let my tears fall.

I've got one cat left. Her name is Haniel. Haniel is said to be the angel of the moon and the grace of God. She's part-goddess and helps us deal with the cycles of life. So Haniel is the perfect companion to help us through this transition to a life without Ralph.

I know there is a divine plan unfolding, and I just have to trust it. For all I know, it may include someone who is the messenger of an angel, someone who is connected to the angelic realm.

Has someone like that ever shown up in your life? It can be someone you end up knowing for a while or someone who simply sits next to you on a train one afternoon. Let me tell you about one such angel messenger whose story really touched me.

The Messengers' Messenger

*"The way people come into your life when you
need them, it's wonderful, and it happens in so
many ways. It's like having an angel. Somebody
comes along and helps you get right."*

STEVIE RAY VAUGHAN

Years ago, a friend of a friend started a kindness challenge in memory of her daughter, who had taken her own life. She encouraged people to engage in random acts of kindness.

One woman had ridden a bus back and forth to a corporate job in the city every day and often seen a man in his late fifties who'd let his beard and hair overgrow and carried a single plastic reusable shopping bag. He always looked sad, so as part of the random acts of kindness challenge, she decided she'd speak to him.

When she did so, she found out how much a small gesture could mean. It turned out no one had spoken to that man on that bus for the past decade. He was starting to feel there wasn't any point in him being around, and the previous night, he'd actually said to God, "If no one acknowledges me tomorrow, I'm going to take my own life."

I think a person who sets out to engage in a random act of kindness—and follows through—may be the messenger of an angel. For that particular woman, hearing what an impact her small gesture had was a turning point in her life as well. It was an awakening. "I can't live my life the same way from this moment," she said to herself. And though I don't know the rest of the story, I would bet you anything her life changed from that moment on.

And so the messenger was as touched as the man who had been on the cusp of taking his own life. And that is one of the beautiful things about this world of communicating with angels—*everyone* involved in the conversation is touched by it. Everyone's life is changed. As we're brought closer together in this communion, the good feeling ripples outward, reaching places it has never reached before.

Where might you find an angel messenger today? How could you be one yourself?

♦

You don't just have to call on angels—you can
attract them through your good deeds.

One way to get closer to angels and messengers of angels is to surround yourself with light and be the light yourself. Let's spend a little time thinking about what that means.

Be the Light

There's a message we can all receive from angels, I think, and it's about how to be the light. I often tell people to be the light when they're trying to make contact with an angel. Sometimes this advice involves imagining yourself surrounded by golden light. Other times it's more metaphorical. I like to say to people, "Hold the light." What do you imagine when you hear that phrase?

Hold the light.

It's got a kind of magic to it, right?

I've got some close friends who are having a real hard time at the moment. A close friend of theirs recently took her own life, and things have been really challenging in their work situation. So these days I often think, *How can I hold the light for them at this moment when everything feels like it's falling apart?* I know I can't hold something back from crumbling, whether it's a romantic relationship or a life's dream. So, it's not helpful to pretend that everything will be okay. But what I can do is be the person who holds out for something positive to happen eventually. I can acknowledge that things are really shit right now, but I can also anchor into hope, perhaps when no one else can. I can be the one who holds out for a miracle.

———————————— ◆ ————————————

If you need a miracle, ask yourself what you
can do to prepare for one unfolding.

Maybe this is something you can be as well—the one who anchors into hope, the one who holds out for a miracle. Is there a situation where you might be able to do that? Is there a friend or a family member who is really struggling now? Surely no one can fault you for trying.

It's important to say that being the light isn't trying to make anyone change what they feel. It isn't trying to take away someone's experience, but it is saying, "I'm going to hold out for a miraculous happening for you."

In kundalini yoga we call it *radiance.* It's an energy that is generated from a consistent spiritual practice and it is imagined as a halo of light around the top of the head, similar to the one you often see in images of saints or deities. The idea is that through a deep-rooted spiritual connection, you hold within your aura this light that emanates from within, and it reaches out and touches everyone that you love and everyone that comes into your life. It is believed by many practitioners that this energy is what magnetizes blessings to you, and it can be contagious to those to whom you are connected.

In Jiu-Jitsu class the other day the brown belt (second highest belt), who often covers for the lead coach, told me that I was the only white belt (lowest belt) whose name he knew.

I asked, "Why is that?" (You know me, I'm always in the spirit of inquiry.)

"You always come here with such a positive energy—it's noticeable, and we really like having you here at the gym," he explained.

"Aww, that's so nice," I said.

"Don't let that go to your head though, you're still a white belt in here!" he said, giving me a wink.

Basically, though still a white belt, there's a light I'm learning how to embody and—hopefully—pass along. In this process, I'm grateful for the support of angels, whether that support comes as a whisper or as a sign so obvious I can't ignore it, like picking the same card from the deck day after day after day. (This has been happening to me lately. I'll tell you about that card at the end of the book. It's a bit uncanny.)

When I started doing "the angel stuff," and especially in my early twenties, once I began to meet success and make a name for myself, a lot of the guys who used to mock me in school came up to me and apologized. "Sorry I used to give you such a hard time," they would say, giving me a handshake or fist bump. They also acknowledged that Mum had been raising me as a single mother and it hadn't been easy. These guys had heard that I was using my money to contribute to the family home and give back. They could see I was trying to do something positive with the good fortune I'd come into, and they let me know they appreciated it. Saying they were sorry for tormenting me when I was young and letting me know they respected what I was doing with my life, even if they didn't quite go for "the angel stuff"—they let me know that too!—was also a way to be the light.

I didn't feel angry with any of those guys. I don't even know if I felt angry with them when they were bullying me. I had found a way to surround myself with light, to try to be the light, and that had protected me and carried me through.

Plus, my vulnerability wasn't all bad; in fact, I think it was a big part of why encountering angels came somewhat easily to me. Through the years I've sometimes asked myself, "Why did I see the angel that day at the barbecue when no one else could see it?" The answer has gradually become clear—I didn't just see the angel, the angel saw me. I was allowing myself to be seen. I was fully revealed. There was no shield, no barrier. Has there been a time when you were able to access some kind of clarity because there was no shield or barrier for you?

♦ ♦ ♦

Archangel Michael is always a good one for us to call on when we're looking to be the light (plus he comes with his own shield). "He Who Is Like God" is also known as "the Prince of Light."

I guess he is the most famous of all the angels for a number of reasons, but mainly because he is known as the supreme protector. This is due to the biblical story where Michael removes the misbehaving angel, Lucifer, from God's kingdom. The Catholic Church therefore sees Michael as a protector against evil, while the modern spiritual movement views the story in a more metaphorical light, seeing Michael as the angel who can protect us from negativity or the ego, which is sometimes pictured as a devil on our shoulder.

———————————— ♦ ————————————

**Archangel Michael is the saint of protection
whose heavenly role is to help us feel safe.**

————————————————————————————

For whatever reason, Michael was the angel that became the most intriguing to me. I know this is the case for many who are exploring the subject of angels. I believe that this is a common theme because we all have a deep longing to feel safe and protected, and so to have a holy figure available to us at all times feels reassuring.

I remember the first time I attended a Mind Body Soul convention in Glasgow. I woke up early to get the train from Greenock to the city—on my own, aged 15 (a lot of stuff happened at age 15!)—and with my pocket money I bought a little laminated image of Archangel Michael. I started taking this image everywhere, and whenever I did readings or spiritual stuff, I set it out as a reminder that Michael was nothing more than a prayer away.

Of course he's right there with you, too. He can help you welcome in new energy and let go of what is no longer serving you. He can help you as you usher positive change into your life, welcome more light, and prepare to begin receiving angel messages.

Perhaps Archangel Michael can also help you cut the cords holding you to the past—a necessary task when welcoming new versions of yourself. I've incorporated a "cut the cords" prayer into my spiritual practice. Here it is.

ANGEL PRAYER TO CUT THE CORDS

Within the spiritual community, cords are seen as energetic bonds that can hold us back or keep us connected to negative energy. They can drain away our life-force and stop us from progressing positively with our life.

When I share this prayer on social media, it always generates such a powerful response and I believe that is because all of us sometimes find ourselves being held back by the ideas, opinions, and negative impressions of others, which can feel like superglue holding us in spaces and places that we no longer want to be in or be connected with.

If you're feeling stuck, unsure, or even replaying something over and over in your mind, I can guarantee that there is a cord binding you to a negative situation or energy and it is affecting your capacity to create love, freedom, and joy in your life. As you are the keeper of your energy, you can actively choose to disconnect from these energies, and angels are always on hand to help you.

As you say this prayer, imagine that powerful angelic forces are swirling around you and pulling out of your energy all the bonds and connections that are holding you back.

It's important to say that the bonds of love that connect you to your loved ones can never be cut or broken. They will always remain. This prayer only cuts negative cords.

Thank you, Archangel Michael, for cutting the unnecessary cords that bind me to people, places, situations, fears, stories, dramas, or anything else that's standing in the way of my greatness.

I make way for miracles.

I make way for light.

I make way for freedom.

And so it is.

Releasing what isn't favorable is just as important as calling in what will be favorable. One makes space for the other.

Talking about space brings me to how important it is to maintain your own. I think you'll soon start to see just how essential boundaries are.

Boundaries

Setting boundaries can be tough. Especially for those of us who tend to be gentle and concerned about others' feelings (as well as quite sensitive with our own). I've learned, however, that setting boundaries is protective. For example, when I'm giving a presentation, I can't let someone take over the conversation to the point where the rest of the audience miss out on the experience I want them to have. This goal requires me to be a bit harsh sometimes. If something is affecting the environment in a way that isn't serving the group, it's up to me to step in, right? Let me give you an example.

One time I was doing a lecture at Kripalu retreat center in Massachusetts and a woman claimed an energy was coming over her. She was jolting and shaking in her chair in a similar way to the people you see in extreme Baptist churches when the preacher comes close to them. I knew that this behavior wasn't a genuine spiritual sensation, more a call for attention. During the retreat the woman had already spoken over other students, given her opinion quite forcefully, and asked questions in the middle of lectures, disrupting the general wellbeing of the group.

I've had a lot of experience of dealing with this kind of thing, especially in appearances at "non-spiritual" events, where I would often get heckled and have to deal with interruptions. I asked the woman to stop and prioritized the good of the group over her need for attention. This kind of assertiveness is tied to the ability to say "no." I've become really good at saying "no." I say "no" to 99 per cent of the invitations I get.

The reason I want you to start thinking about your own boundaries and ability to say "no" is that this will help make the space in your life to start noticing the messages angels may be trying to give. Saying "no" gives you the time and presence of mind to notice signs. (*More on these in Chapter 10.*) When you notice one, thank the angels for reminding you of their presence. Thank them for showing up in your life. Then thank yourself for giving them the room to make themselves known.

Keeping your boundaries in place also shows you are willing to have an experience with an angel. Saying "no" to an event you don't want to attend can be saying "yes" to a meeting with an angel instead.

◆ ◆ ◆

Let's turn the tables now and think about what it's like for an angel to meet us and spend time with us. What do they see and feel in our presence? We can be light. We can be uplifting. We can use gratitude, affirmations, meditation, and other practices to be someone who uplifts others, the way that angels do. We can be authentically ourselves, in service to others, praising the divine, loving—well, loving everyone. (*More on these four pillars of angelic connection in Chapter 7.*)

If you can model yourself on angels, you're more likely to gain the benefits of their company. Aspire to be like them. Remember, like attracts like.

———————— ◆ ————————

In order to experience angels more, we just
have to become more like them.

Angels will always see the good in you. You can be in the darkest night of the soul and they'll still see your fullest potential. You might have done the craziest of deeds, but they'll still hold you in the highest esteem. You may have just a fraction of the "perfect Child of God," as Jesus calls it in the Gnostic texts, within you and they'll see it.

◆ ◆ ◆

Okay, so to review a little bit, because we've covered a lot here. Angels are messengers. They can send their messages to us in many ways, including through other people. We can get closer to them by trying to be like them, holding the light. They protect us and guide us through the challenges of our lives. We need to put boundaries in place to give ourselves the best opportunity to spend time with them. And they see our strength, power, and goodness. It's really powerful to imagine yourself the way angels see you, with grace and light. Their presence will help you stay present. They have been present on Earth since the beginning of time.

·5·

Angels through the Ages

"Angels, in the early morning
May be seen the Dews among,
Stooping—plucking—smiling—flying—
Do the Buds to them belong?

Angels, when the sun is hottest
May be seen the sands among,
Stooping—plucking—sighing—flying—
Parched the flowers they bear along."

EMILY DICKINSON

Their miracles are similar. Their names and traditions are different. Yet since the beginning of time, all around the world, there have been beings in all cultures, all traditions, and all religions that are similar to what we know today as angels. Before you could jump on a

75

British Airways flight and get from London to Bangkok in half a day, people around the globe had similar beliefs in unseen beings who moved through the air and helped them.

Over the years, I've received countless requests for proof that angels exist. I think it's obvious I'm not a scientist and I'm not going to pretend I can give concrete proof, but I do believe that something is going on here!

We just need to recognize that angels have been described, named, and experienced differently the world over, but their compassion, love, peace, and kindness have remained the same.

Angels Around the World

Let's look at a few of these, from Australia to Japan to India, Tibet, the United States, the Middle East... I could go on.

Starting in the southern hemisphere, Indigenous Australians had Mimi spirits called *Wandjinas*. Art depicting these supernatural creatures can be found in caves and on rocks in the northwest of Australia in the Kimberley region. *Wandjinas* are part of a creator spirit that can separate itself into individual beings to help bring rain and heal people. In the artwork, their heads are round, their eyes are large and black, and they have no mouth. But perhaps the most interesting thing visually is that there are strands of light stemming off their heads as if they're emanating light. In tribal creation stories, these "sky-beings" originally descended to Earth from the Milky Way.

These depictions really strike me, given that the first angel I saw looked like light with dark, hollow eyes. It was about 10 years after that barbecue reading that I first saw pictures of the *Wandjinas*.

In the Japanese tradition, the "Shinto gods" are the *Kami*, "good spirits," who are said to move through the air as if they have wings, although they're not said to have wings. I quite like that. If you look in the Bible, there are only a few instances where angels have wings. In most cases in Scripture, they disguise themselves as human-like beings and announce themselves as angels.

Shinto practitioners will pray to *Kami*, petition them, and hope they will be able to answer their prayers. Humans can transform into *Kami* after death. Followers of Shintoism and Buddhism also hang prayers written on little wooden plaques called *Ema* for the *Kami* to find. This practice feels similar to those of Native American tribes, who hang dreamcatchers to resist negative energy and bring good energy.

Buddhism also has angel-like beings called bodhisattvas. Do you know that Uma Thurman's dad, Robert Thurman, is an Indo-Tibetan Buddhism scholar? At one time he was also a Buddhist monk. In his book *Essential Tibetan Buddhism*, he describes the bodhisattvas as "the archangelic beings of Buddhism."

Bodhi means "enlightenment" and *sattva* is "true expression" or "purity," so these are beings of enlightened truth and clear expression. They are either already enlightened or moving toward enlightenment. They can be both ethereal and living, and they are dedicated to the service of all other sentient beings.

According to Buddhist tradition, Avalokiteshvara, the lord of compassion, was looking down upon the land and when he saw people suffering, he cried tears of compassion. The tears fell from the sky and hit the mud, and from the mud came lotus flowers that birthed beings of brilliance and light. These beings reached out to those suffering and dedicated themselves to liberating them from it entirely. They were bodhisattvas.

People pray to bodhisattvas, chant to invoke them, and light candles as well. You might even know some of these beings—Green Tara is one of them.

Another cool thing that has really influenced my teaching is that the way to invoke a bodhisattva is to become more like one. In the Mahayana tradition of Buddhism, the goal is to become a bodhisattva by exiting the wheel of karma and entering a place of light and brightness.

Both Hindu and Buddhist traditions have a deity called Garuda, who is known as the king of birds or lord of birds. This divine being is depicted as a sort of cross between a human and an eagle.

Those of you who study yoga might know *Garudasana*, or Eagle Pose, a standing pose that is a bit challenging. From *Tadasana*, Mountain Pose, standing up straight with your arms raised to the sky, fingers touching, you bend your knees a bit and wrap one leg around the other. Then you wrap one arm around the other, hold them up in front of your face, and balance! Now hold it for as long as you can. (You can try it later.)

Another intriguing deity in Hinduism is Krishna, the god of compassion and love, who is often depicted with blue skin. As told in the Bhagavad Gita, he appeared as a spiritual guide to a great warrior named Arjuna, who was praying to Vishnu for help. Similar to an angel, Krishna is an expression of God, what is called an "avatar" in Hinduism, but not God himself entirely.

Over in the canyons of what is now called Utah, in the United States, beginning perhaps thousands of years ago, hunter-gatherers carved and painted large figures with a human shape. (Quick cave art refresher for those who need it: Pictographs are painted, and petroglyphs are carved. Super useful if you're planning a National Park vacay in the American West anytime soon.) The hollow or missing eyes give these figures a spooky appearance and immediately bring to mind the indigenous Australian art I discussed above, not to mention my first angel sighting at the barbecue.

In Horseshoe Canyon in Canyonlands National Park, one figure towers over the others, with dramatic round missing eyes (while the other figures appear to be fully painted in) and enormously broad shoulders, or possibly a cape (or wings). This figure is known as the Barrier Canyon Holy Man. It looks as though he's floating.

Buckhorn Wash, also in Utah, features some supernatural-looking rock art as well. These figures appear to guard the San Rafael river and some visitors call them "rain angels."

Thanking spirits, for rain and many other things, is a practice that also can be found across the world. In the Celtic tradition, the Druids, the shamanic priests, had a deep reverence for the natural world. They would call upon the spirits of a particular landscape, such as a forest or river, and offer thanks for being welcomed into their space and time. Rituals seeking protection and spiritual direction would follow. The Celts would also look to natural forms for guidance and answers to their prayers.

On the other side of the world, on Hawai'i's Big Island, the native people, the Kānaka Maoli, ask for the blessing of the goddess Pele when they enter her landscape. Pele is the goddess of volcanoes and believed to reside at the top of the volcano Kilauea.

The Mesopotamian people had beings called the Apkallu, "the wise," who were winged deities with human bodies and either human or eagle heads. These beings have been thought of as the precursors to angels. Artwork depicts them protecting the king and nature, and being involved in ritualistic activity. I find it fascinating how much this recalls the descriptions of angels which were shared through the vision of Ezekiel in the Bible.

Ezekiel was a priest and prophet in Jerusalem in the sixth century BCE, but his angelic encounter took place while he was in captivity in Babylon. Jerusalem had fallen and the Temple had been destroyed. The Hebrew nation had been forced out of Israel, and five years into exile, things seemed a little desperate.

Sitting next to a canal on his 30th birthday, Ezekiel had a vision, and because of it he was able to give the group of refugees around him hope that they would return to Israel one day and build a new temple. (If you haven't heard, they did, and it lasted quite a while, until the Romans destroyed it in 70 CE and the Jews were once again forced out.)

So, what did Ezekiel see?

I looked, and I saw a windstorm coming out of the north—an immense cloud with flashing lightning and surrounded by brilliant light. The center of the fire looked like glowing metal, and in the fire was what looked like four living creatures. In appearance their form was human, but each of them had four faces and four wings. Their legs were straight; their feet were like those of a calf and gleamed like burnished bronze. Under their wings on their four sides they had human hands. All four of them had faces and wings, and the wings of one touched the wings of another. Each one went straight ahead; they did not turn as they moved.

Their faces looked like this: Each of the four had the face of a human being, and on the right side each had the face of a lion, and on the left the face of an ox; each also had the face of an eagle. Such were their faces. They each had two wings spreading out upward, each wing touching that of the creature on either side; and each had two other wings covering its body. Each one went straight ahead. Wherever the spirit would go, they would go, without turning as they went. The appearance of the living creatures was like burning coals of fire or like torches. Fire moved back and forth among the creatures; it was bright, and lightning flashed out of it. The creatures sped back and forth like flashes of lightning.[1]

Pretty incredible, right? An angel with six wings and four faces—an eagle, a child, a bull, and a lion. And angels appearing in spheres of light, little orbs. These show up in photographs now all the time. You've probably seen them many times.

The exiles may have felt that they were far from God's dwelling spot in the now-ruined Temple, but God was showing them pretty clearly that He wasn't limited to any one location. He was with them along the canal in Babylon, just like he'd been with them in Jerusalem. Unbound.

Different names, different traditions, but there's a throughline that carries us from the remote wilderness of Australia to the Krishna-worshippers on the colorful streets of Jaipur. The similarities across these traditions help us establish that angelic encounters have happened for thousands of years.

Renaissance Angel Imagery

All the images I have described above helped give birth to the Renaissance angel imagery we all know today.

In the 15th century, Andrea del Verrocchio sculpted "Little Angel with Dolphin"—a naked little boy with wings, plump cheeks, and wavy hair (and a dolphin). Spanish painter Bartolomé Bermejo painted "Saint Michael Triumphs over the Devil" in the same century, depicting Michael as a warrior with wings that were red, gold, and a blackish color. Michael is raising his sword above his head and looks quite human. Also around this time, Italian painter Filippo Lippi depicted angels as human-like with golden wings and curly blond hair.

Painted around 1522, Rosso Fiorentino's "Musical Angel," who is playing the lute, has red hair with white wings that have reddish feathers on both sides. The artist himself had red hair, so it's easy to see what likely influenced that decision.

Along the bottom of "The Sistine Madonna" by Raphael from the mid-16th century are two childlike angels (cherubs) with wings in a sort of resting position. When you look more closely, you'll see many angel faces surrounding Mary, who is holding Christ.

Angels are everywhere in the masterpieces of Italian painter Sandro Botticelli, looking like beautiful humans with white wings.

In 1597 Michelangelo Caravaggio painted his angel in "Rest on the Flight into Egypt" as a young white male, mostly nude, with black wings.

These Renaissance and early Baroque artists made angels more palatable. Since it was hard to know how a creature was moving through the air, maybe people said, "We'll give it wings." No surprise European artists often gave angels blond hair and blue eyes, pushing the narrative colonizers wanted in place. In turn, the angels we see in art and in films today are actually a product of the Renaissance period.

But, as you already know, angels come in all shapes and sizes.

Angels Are for Everyone

We all look different, right? Pop me in the middle of Takeshita Street in Tokyo and I'll be a foot taller than most people. I'll be whiter, I'll be burlier, I'll probably have more tattoos. But I'll still be human and so will all the people around me. And it's the same with angels— whatever their names and forms, they help us embrace a diversity we should celebrate.

After a tornado killed her parents, Ari Hallmark, known as "the girl who saw angels," described the angel she saw as extremely tall with long blond hair. The creature was "young and beautiful and healthy"[2] and the girl found it hard to tell if it was a man or a woman. What stood out was a feeling of "caring." In *The Girl Who Saw Heaven: A fateful tornado and a journey of faith*, we are given more insight into her experience. "I don't remember a lot of sounds in Heaven, so with my angel it was more like, when she would communicate something, I could feel what she was saying without her actually saying it."[3] The six-year-old saw other angels as well and drew what she had seen when she returned to Earth.

There are unseen beings out there. And they're here to help us. However they may appear. You might see a haze that is an indistinct color or a creature that resembles a bird, but they're the same essence. They're there for you. Your religion, your skin color, your sexual orientation don't matter—angels are for you. Angels are for everyone.

When I started to do a little digging, looking into the anthropology of spiritual beings, I realized that I had to bring something about all these fascinating forms and historical similarities into my teaching. I made a pact to myself that my work was going to be about diversity. In my proposal for *Angel Prayers* in 2013, my main teaching was diversity among angels. I was inspired by the *Kami*, the cave paintings, the devotion to Krishna. My research inspired me to make angels as inclusive as possible, belonging to everyone, just as they had throughout the centuries. I wanted everyone to feel called and connected to them, not just those who bore an outward resemblance to the way the Renaissance painters chose to depict them.

At the time I was using someone else's angel cards. Every single angel on them was white. I did a reading for a Black woman and felt uneasy turning over the cards. Not a single one represented who she was.

Another time I was doing a reading on Skype and the theme was mother healing—healing the mother line. I closed my eyes, asking loved ones and angels to come forward for this woman who had never felt loved and cherished by her mother. In my mind, I asked the angels, *How can we heal that for this woman?*

The angels brought forward the soul of a beloved Black maid named Annabel. When I told her, the woman for whom I was doing the reading (who happened to be white) started crying. "That's who raised me," she said.

She had come from a wealthy family where nannies raised the children, and she had adored her nanny, Annabel, but when it came time to move on, she had never got to see or speak to her again, and she'd never recovered from the rupture. Instead, she'd been wandering through life without any closure on the relationship she'd had with the woman who had been the most important person in her life.

When I first saw my guardian angel, I knew the fact that he was Black was a message for me. It's not that I'm here to speak for anyone, more that I can make my work approachable and accessible to everyone. So, I asked that we changed the way the angels looked for my own oracle cards. We had to represent every skin tone, every shape and size, every age. The message was: "It doesn't matter who you are, no one's been forgotten."

In fact, I often used to say, "In the eyes of angels, we're all equal," but with the rise of Black Lives Matter and the Me Too movements, that remark didn't seem to be enough. Last summer I discussed the topic with my friend the psychologist Dr. Deborah Egerton, an expert on diversity, when I was doing a bunch of inner work on ensuring my teachings and intentions were aligned with my actions. "Dr. E.," as we lovingly called her, guided me to call in the angels to share a new way of getting my point across. I did so, and received the message: "Love has forgotten no one." *Bam!* That's my new introduction.

We all come from different backgrounds and have different experiences. But we all come from the same presence and will return to that presence, the presence that angels emanate from too. That presence is Love, and of course Love has forgotten no one.

Our role on Earth is to find within ourselves and in our lives where we haven't let Love reach, and change that. Our work on Earth will never be done until the truth that Love has forgotten no one becomes a reality. That's what it means to create heaven on Earth.

There are so many ways the divine can show itself to us. I can't tell you how it's going to appear in your life. That's up to you to discover. But I know it will. No one has been forgotten.

Now that we've had a bit of an anthropology lesson and talked about why I'm so committed to diversity in depictions of angels, I'd like to tell a couple more stories about how angels have appeared, this time in the 21st century.

21st-Century Angel Encounters

One evening in early November I was on my way to Mauchline, a small village close to the River Ayr where the famous poet Robert Burns once lived. I remember the night so clearly. I had been writing for the *Scottish Sun* for about a year, so I guess I was around 21, and I was set to give a presentation on angels along with readings in a members' club raising funds for a school soccer team. If I remember correctly, I was filling in for another psychic. I didn't love doing these events, but it was a good way to get myself out there. I would get a flat fee and it would raise money for the club. Except I lost my way on a country road. This was before GPS, and when you were lost, you were lost. So, there I was on this dark narrow road, thinking, *Oh shit! I've no idea where I am.*

I remember saying, "Angels, thank you so much for sending a clear sign that I should go to this event and also the direction I should go in."

At that moment I saw an elderly woman in the distance just coming up the side of the road. She was in complete darkness other than the light from my headlights, and I thought, *That's really weird.* Obviously, with a little old woman, I wasn't concerned about my safety, but it was a bit odd nonetheless.

The woman got closer and closer and I just watched her. She had curled, blow-dried hair and was wearing a little blue padded rain jacket.

Finally she came up to the car and tapped on the window.

"You okay in there?" she asked in a broad Scottish accent.

"I'm actually lost," I told her, rolling down the window. "I can't find this place here."

I showed her where I was trying to go on the map.

"Oh, I know where that is," she said in a relaxed manner.

She told me where to go and as I was folding away the map, I turned to thank her and she'd gone.

I stuck my head out of the car and looked round. There was nowhere to go but along the road in one direction or the other, and I didn't see her in either.

Did I just have an encounter with an angel? I thought.

I had a tough crowd that night and kept the story to myself, but I've thought about it many times since.

A client of mine had an experience in France that made her wonder the same thing. She had recently retired and was treating herself by going on a Catholic pilgrimage. One afternoon she went to visit Mont-Saint-Michel, off the Normandy coast. During her free time she wandered away from the abbey down a side street, and when it was time to regroup, she couldn't find a way to get back inside it. She found herself getting nervous as she searched for a way back in, as it was starting to get really dark and she was a woman alone abroad.

She tried to open the gates to the abbey to take shelter, but they were locked. Desperately, she looked around, thinking, *Dear God, send me a messenger. Help me find my way.*

Then she felt a hand on her shoulder. She turned and looked into the eyes of an Italian-looking guy with beautiful dark hair.

He said, "Michael," and pointed to an opening in the gates the woman hadn't seen. She thanked him and hurried inside.

Appearing out of nowhere, two people helping lost strangers find their way.

Angels—if that's what these were, I'll let you decide—can help people who feel lost metaphorically as well.

One woman in Southern California felt absolutely devastated after her dog passed away. She felt so lonely walking on the beach without him. One day, she was standing with her feet in the ocean thinking, *I just need to know that you're okay*, when out of nowhere a golden retriever appeared, on its own, the owner nowhere in sight. It ran over to the woman, who started to pet it.

On its collar, she found one word: "Angel."

A bull, an eagle, a lion, a child. A little old lady with blow-dried hair. A handsome Italian man. A dog on a beach. They're here to help. They're here to point the way. They're here to bring rain to a country in drought. Here to heal a woman fighting the cancer overtaking her body. Here to tell a girl who has lost her family that she'll see them again. They're here. That's the central message I want to give you now.

If you've read some of my earlier books, you may remember detailed descriptions of the different angels and their colors, auras, personalities, and strengths. The Myriam with their white light. Raziel with his golden aura. Chamuel with his piercing blue eyes. I was often super specific, for example telling you how Uriel can help the self-employed and is also associated with men's health. Earlier in my career, I was going along with what I was being told. I was the new guy, the young guy, the one trying to make it, sometimes being heckled on stage. I still do call on specific angels—I call on Archangel Michael every day, and to help my dad out with a work situation I called on Raphael—but the whole point of writing this book is to make angels as approachable and accessible as possible, and if people feel they have to memorize an encyclopedia on auras and energies, they may miss out on the essential benefit to our relationship with angels.

So, here I just want to say that connecting with angels is easy and you don't need me.

———————————— ♦ ————————————

There are billions of angels "out there," but just
by saying, "My angel," you call yours to you.

————————————————————————

If you just say, "Hey, any angel out there, thank you," it'll be enough. If you forget about Azrael's chiseled chin or how to say his name in Arabic, it doesn't matter. Depictions of angels have changed through the ages, but your angel has been there through all of them, and even before that.

You can say, "It feels so good to know I'm connected to my angel."

And so it is.

·6·

The Spiritual Laws

"The most beautiful and profound emotion we
can experience is the sensation of the mystical.
It is at the root of all true science. That deeply
emotional conviction of the presence of a
superior reasoning power which is revealed in the
incomprehensible Universe is my idea of God."

ALBERT EINSTEIN

One night in early June I was doing the Angel Team Live call I do on the first Sunday of every month. At the end of every call, I take on three people live and do a reading for each one in front of the rest of the group, usually about 400 people live with up to 1,300 watching the replay. To select these three people, I open up the list of participants, close my eyes, run up and down the guest list with my mouse, and just let it stop on random names. Each person I pick gets to ask a question.

When I started talking to the first woman—somewhere in the US—I got the feeling that when she was near water, she felt connected. In my mind I was conjuring a big body of water like the sea or a lake.

"Oh, that's my pool," the woman nodded her head.

But I knew it was something more than a swimming pool, so I let myself stay with the image. I closed my eyes. When I'm in these conversations, I just trust what comes to me and know that it means something, even if we don't always know what at the time.

"When I go to the water, there's a man waiting for you there," I told the woman.

"Oh my God," she exclaimed, "that's my late husband! He was a sea captain."

When a woman came on for the final reading, I was pleasantly surprised that she was speaking in a Scottish accent. When I speak publicly, I tend to clean up my Glaswegian (Weejie) accent so that people from far and wide can understand what I'm saying. But as soon as I hear another Scottish accent, I can't help but relax and my own accent gets broader and thicker as well.

As I do with everyone who comes on, I asked the woman her name and where she came from. She told me her name was Sharon and that she was "just through the tunnel from you." She went on to explain, "I live next to Rouken Glen Park." Rouken Glen is a giant park in the south of

Glasgow. I knew it well because I'd been there several times to walk the dogs and also attend the public rituals celebrating many of the Celtic festivals held by a group called the Druids of Caledon.

"How long have you been a member of Angel Team?" I asked.

"Since the beginning. But I actually had a reading from you nineteen years ago in Isobel Knox's kitchen."

I should add that I had no idea who Isobel was, but I guessed she was someone who had hosted an angel readings party—the gatherings I would attend in people's homes during the early days of my career.

"Oh my God," I said. "I must have been so young!"

"You *were* very young, but let me tell you, it was the best reading I've ever had!"

I welled up with emotion. It was touching to hear that someone had followed my journey as long as Sharon had.

"So, how can I help you today?" I asked. "What's your question?"

"I have loved learning about spirituality and sharing it with others," Sharon said, "but I've lost my confidence in it, and it's because I don't feel healed that I wonder if I can help heal anyone. I want to know if this is the right path for me, Kyle."

At that point, I closed my eyes and thanked the angels for bringing through messages of clarity for Sharon to hear. I picked one of my angel cards for her and it was Archangel Raphael, *Clarity of Vision*.

Like always, I just let whatever comes to me flow through. "Before I do the reading, I want to share something important," I said. "You don't have to be fully healed to heal others. I really believe the wounded can heal! *A Course in Miracles* says, 'When I am healed, I am not healed alone!' and what I believe is that through sharing healing with others, we can also receive it for ourselves. *A Course in Miracles* also says, 'To teach is to learn,' and so I think one of the clearest ways to become more connected to angels is through sharing them with others."

Then I could feel the angels around Sharon beginning to give me impressions of her energy. I could see her being the strong and together one of the family, the person that everyone else relied on. Even though this might feel like a heavy load to carry, I could sense that it gave her a feeling of place and purpose in the world.

I shared what I was finding out and Sharon told me it was accurate.

"I feel you've always been a confident person," I went on. "You've never been one to doubt yourself and so the reason you're feeling so unsure now is because this isn't in your nature."

Internally I asked, *So why is this happening to Sharon?* and then out of nowhere I had a vision of her in a circle of women. It looked as though they were all interested in spiritual work, but one of them seemed to have a dislike for Sharon. I could see this woman telling her something to the effect that she wasn't ready and I could tell that this had made an impact on her.

"Someone else has got into your head," I told her, "and this is what's affecting your confidence and making you doubt yourself."

"That makes total sense, yes!" Sharon replied.

"I actually think she's placed the evil eye on you!"

"It feels like that to me, too!"

The evil eye is when someone sends negative energy your way and will do anything and everything they can to make your life a misery. Not everyone who casts the evil eye knows that they're essentially infiltrating your auric field with negativity, but there are people out there who are doing this intentionally, and we call them "psychic vampires."

Unfortunately, it's very common for those who are less successful to try to hold back those who are more spiritually gifted.

I explained what I was discovering to Sharon. "Archangel Raphael, the angel whose name means 'God heals,' is the angel of healing, but just as importantly, he's the angel who can help us see clearly," I told her. "Someone else's ideas of you have clouded your vision and you're believing their story rather than your truth."

Sharon looked thoughtful.

"Your angels are here to help you see this situation clearly," I continued, "and to know that you are absolutely deserving of a spiritual connection and more than capable of sharing it with others. You need to continue doing this."

I paused to let Sharon process the information and then posed a question.

"Are you willing to release the false narratives that others have placed in your energy?"

"I am," she replied.

It was time to thank the angels again. And that's exactly what I did, out loud. "Thank you, angels, for removing these foreign ideas and ill intentions from Sharon's aura with immediate effect! Thank you for cloaking her in a golden light of love and safety."

I then talked a little about how important it was to be in community and Sharon agreed. At that point another clear image came to me. This one was of a scar running down someone's chest.

"Do you know someone with a big scar down their chest?" I asked.

Sharon nodded. "It's my best friend's sister," she said. "She's also a friend of mine. She's had open-heart surgery and has a huge scar from it."

Speaking of community, it seemed clear to me that there was room to strengthen one here.

"I feel that person wants to be a bigger part of your world," I told Sharon. "You've got to get closer to her. There's a presence here that's trying to bring you together."

Sharon didn't seem surprised in the least. "She's terminal," she said, "and she claims she has no beliefs." She filled me in a bit more. "Her sister's very religious, but this lady, she doesn't believe in anything spiritual. She *aggressively* doesn't believe. Yet I think she's calling for help."

We both understood that this woman saw religion and spirituality as weaknesses. Nonetheless, something really powerful was happening on the call. So much so that I felt my hair standing on end.

"She's really in her final days," Sharon continued, "and she's desperate to get something to help her. To give her some calm."

I let Sharon know she didn't even need to be spiritual about this mission. If she could just be with this woman, spend time with her, I thought there might be a spiritual awakening for them both. All she had to do, in other words, was be of service, and the Universe would take care of the rest.

You could see Sharon's mood get lighter as she received this message. This task turned her from focusing on all the ways things weren't fair to her at the moment to how she could be a companion to a woman who was suffering and at the end of her life.

A few days before this call, I'd seen that 30 Seconds to Mars, Jared Leto's band, who I'd loved when I was a teenager, would be in town soon. I called Robyn, who'd been a friend of mine since we were in biology class together, and said we should get tickets. Well, a few days after that astonishing Angel Team Live call, I found out from Robyn that we were on the guest list through a connection of hers whose mother was apparently my biggest fan.

The band were playing at the Hydro, Glasgow's largest concert venue. It looks like a big UFO and changes color at night! At the entrance I got a wristband with the number 00444, which was a bit odd, as Robyn had got the wristband just before and her number was 00334. These numbers usually go in sequence, don't they? For those of you who don't know, 444 is *the* angel number.

———————————— ♦ ————————————

Seeing the number 444 is a message that
you are surrounded by angels.

Robyn invited Kiara, the woman who'd got us on the list, to come by and say hi after the show. I wanted to thank her for being so generous. When we met up, guess what she said? "So, you gave my mum a reading the other day! Do you remember telling her about the scar down her friend's chest?"

Kiara's mother was *Sharon*, the woman from the call that Sunday night!

I don't know if Sharon and the lady with the scar have got closer. I hope they have. From what Sharon told me, it sounded clear that the woman with the scar hadn't asked for help from angels, but they were certainly swooping in to support her nonetheless. Could it be that someone had called on the *Divine Law of Grace* for this woman? Or could it be that the *Divine Law of Compensation* was at work? Now feels as good a time as any to discuss these two laws and how they work.

I think of these laws as guidelines. They haven't been handed down on scrolls; they are basically what I've found works as I've developed my intuition and worked to improve my communication with angels. I'll give you both laws here:

1. *The Divine Law of Grace*: We can help bring grace to other people.

2. *The Divine Law of Compensation*: When we serve, we are served in return.

They're both quite beautiful laws and together they will help us better understand our connection to the divine. Let's look at them in turn, starting with the Divine Law of Grace.

The Divine Law of Grace

We can help bring grace to other people

Based on everything we've learned about angels to this point, we know they cannot help us unless we ask for help. And indeed, this is the main teaching out there, based on the concept of free will. In short, we have a choice. We get to decide if we want to accept help or not. I think this is true, yet I've always had a question around that belief. (As you may have noticed, I have a question around almost everything.)

Here's where things get tricky for me—so many people have had angel experiences or encounters where they were saved or supported even though they hadn't asked for help. Perhaps you've had one yourself, or know of someone who has. You're about to step onto the road, you don't see a car hurtling along, and an unseen hand seems to come and sweep you back. If you're like me, you might ask, "Why was I saved, given that I never asked?"

This is where the Divine Law of Grace comes in. What if your soul said a prayer for you? Perhaps in your conscious mind, you didn't say anything, but your soul sent off a little SOS. Or perhaps someone else was looking out for you, perhaps acting like the messenger of an angel. Either way, the car speeding along was maybe about to stop you from fulfilling other missions or experiencing outcomes you had started to create, but you were saved by grace.

Grace gives a second chance. It gives a place to breathe. It forgives. It drops defenses. It protects. It reveals. It chooses spirit over fear.

It brings angels to the place where they're most needed. It gives without taking. It is more than we could have hoped for. We didn't ask, or perhaps even always deserve, to be granted it. Grace is the essence of angels, if you think about it, and is impossible without divine love.

How did we get lucky enough to be surrounded by supportive, loving beings at all times? I don't have an answer for that, I just know that we are. And I know that grace is also connected to our creations and our manifestations. They hold us as well. They pull us through.

So, I started to call on the Divine Law of Grace when I was praying for people who I knew were maybe going through a hard time. This law is especially useful when I'm praying for someone who can't help themselves—someone who is struggling with addiction, for example. I call on angels through the Divine Law of Grace to guide this person to a space of wholeness or healing. I know that if it's for their highest good, it will happen for them.

◆

Praying in service of someone else
draws angels close.

The person might be able to pray for themselves, but they won't. Perhaps they've become disengaged from their spirituality, or for some other reason they're not in alignment with the angel realm. Like Sharon's friend. Sharon understood that she had a barrier up, but some part of her was looking to bring it down, to welcome in grace.

Do you know someone in your life who isn't in a position to pray for themselves? Or do you know someone who has their defenses up and doesn't want to acknowledge how interconnected we all are? You can call in a moment of grace for that person. You can ask for grace to save them.

Some people truly are saved, healed, or guided because someone else prayed for them. I believe that many of us are saved by grace because of the prayers of our ancestors. Think of someone you once knew who may be gone from this Earth, but whose prayers are likely still protecting you now.

This is one of the things in my work that I've really loved. It feels so uplifting to know this possibility is out there. We don't have to understand exactly how it works to know that it does. It's yet another great reason to live our lives in gratitude. How wonderful is it to be held and supported by the prayers of those who have gone before us?

There's another cool thing to know about the Divine Law of Grace: it shows us how to send help to others without taking on their spiritual journey or lessons. We don't have to become weighed down by what they're going through. (Remember the importance of boundaries.) The Divine Law of Grace gives us space as well. We're not entangling ourselves in their situation and trying to unravel it all, we're just sending love and support their way.

Remember how Sharon put it when she talked about her friend with the scar? She said she was looking for something to "give her some calm." Whether we can meet in person or not, we can bring others some calm.

Now we'll move onto the second law I mentioned, which is, of course, connected to everything we've been talking about already.

The Divine Law of Compensation

When we serve, we are served in return

This law is about building grace into a potent force. Do you remember learning about cumulative totals in maths class? It's a term related to the word "accumulate," where you keep adding on as you go. *The Divine Law of Compensation* looks at the cumulative effect of goodwill and good deeds.

Sometimes all the good you've done in your life will save you. In fact, it can come back to you tenfold. You will be compensated for your compassion. Compassion isn't just a loving energy pouring out of you, but also one coming back to you.

I love to connect people. I took a trip out to LA three years ago and met up with my friends in the personal development field, who are all friends with one another now. Some are in business partnerships as well. One of the best people I know, who I got to know better on that trip, was psychologist and business coach Niyc Pidgeon, whose second book, *One More Day*, came out in September 2024. She mentioned a trip she was taking to Barbados for a retreat, and during a dinner

I hosted, she suggested I join the retreat to teach kundalini yoga and meditation. (We're both dedicated kundalini practitioners. I think that's one of the many reasons we get on so well.)

On the last morning of the retreat we were having breakfast together when Niyc told me about her mission to help people get through dark times using positive psychology. Several of her close friends had taken their own lives, she told me. Leaning in, I wanted to hear more, because something inside of me knew that this was an important life mission. Niyc had mentioned that in the car after one of her friend's funeral services, her close friend Sophie had said to her, "We need to make a pact. We can't let this happen again!" and Niyc had agreed. But only a short time after that, Sophie also died by suicide.

I found myself welling up, looking out over the ocean and the white sands of Sandy Lane. Every hair on my body stood on end when I said, "You can't break the pact. Even though Sophie can't be here to help you, you need to do your part by writing this book and fulfilling this calling!"

I was so certain that angels were coming through for Niyc with her mission. I felt them there with us. Niyc, too, had goosebumps over her body and we held hands, nodding, knowing that this truly was a spiritual calling.

Niyc told me she'd started a proposal, and I let her know she absolutely had to keep going with it. Angels were swooping in to support her. It was such a powerful moment that she wrote about it in her book!

Niyc has become one of my closest friends, but even before that happened, as soon as I was back in the UK I got on the phone to the managing director at Hay House UK to tell her about this important book. Of course she signed it up! Niyc also became the biz coach to a dear friend and helped him quadruple his income in a matter of months. Just by being in her company, I feel more abundant and confident in my own gifts.

I love to make these connections. Partly this is because I live by "the more, the merrier," and to me that's how it feels. But it's also living in accordance with the Divine Law of Compensation and I know I will be helped in return. It's not a transaction—I'll set you up with a great editor and you'll book me for a retreat in the Caribbean. No, the compensation will come from a higher power. I'll support you on your spiritual pathway, which in turn will help me on mine. Angels want us to feel part of something. Angels are connectors too. When we gather, angels gather with us.

**Divine compensation is when all your good
acts come back to bless your life.**

Sometimes the word "karma" comes to mind in this respect, but I've stopped using the word unless I can provide context. The idea comes from Hinduism and is also present in Buddhism. The view is that as we go through life after life, our actions, both good and bad, reverberate back to us until eventually we break the wheel of karma and achieve nirvana—liberation from suffering and the cycle of birth and rebirth. But I don't think everything is exactly that tit for tat. You can't graph it out—this good thing happened because of this; this bad thing happened because of this other thing. I'm really not a fan of "Karma's gonna get you." And I can't possibly agree that a child ever "deserves" to die.

I don't think everything happens for a reason, but I believe we can always find a reason to live, a reason to love, a reason to continue and extend our love further, no matter what the situation. And I believe that the light we put out into the world keeps gathering to become a force of its own.

Making the Most of the Divine Laws

So now that we know there are these beautiful laws in effect—the gentle landing after a fall, and the idea that goodwill comes back to us—what can we do to make these flows of positive energy even more powerful?

I think this work is connected to raising our vibration. The higher our vibration, and therefore the greater our access to our own sense of calm, the more we can give to someone else. The higher our vibration, and therefore the more good energy we put out to the Universe, the more comes back to us.

When we move into a frequency that better aligns with angels, we become vessels for positive energy to pass through and become amplified. How can we do this? It can be as simple as greeting our neighbors, asking a receptionist about her day, showing curiosity about what other people believe, truly listening to what other people have to say, and wishing the best for others.

And perhaps we also need to be truthful about places where we are blocking positive energy. I can think of one right now for myself: I'm not usually quick to respond to anger, but I'm also not the best at receiving compliments. It's like I don't have a shield up when someone wants to attack me, but I put one up when they're offering praise. Go figure! Maybe I need to start responding differently. I thank the angels every time I speak with them. Surely I can thank a person paying me a compliment.

If we want to radiate, if we hope to reach our highest vibration, we should accept any source of light that comes our way. Praise should be received.

Do you know the story of Abraham hosting the angels in Genesis? Right away he gets them some water so they can wash their feet, gives them a shady place to rest, and brings them a beautiful meal. (The meal is prepared by his servants and wife, but to be fair this is the fifth century BCE.)

When we receive light, it's almost as if we're playing host to angels or messengers of angels—greeting them, setting out our best china, pouring them a good cup of tea and bringing them scones fresh out of the oven. "Welcome! I'm glad you're here" this open embrace seems to say. Perhaps we'll even take out our precious angel cards, our first deck, frayed and falling apart and beloved, and ask our guests to pick one.

All of this is connected to authenticity, service, devotion, and love, which happen to be the Four Pillars of Angelic Connection. This is where we can really up our angel game.

·7·

The Four Pillars

"When angels visit us, we do not hear the rustle of wings,
nor feel the feathery touch of the breast of a dove; but we
know their presence by the love they create in our hearts."

MARY BAKER EDDY

I've introduced you to this concept in earlier chapters, but now I'd like to expand on it to give you a better picture of how I see angelic vibration. We know asking for an encounter isn't enough—we need to vibrate at a higher level to experience angels. To do that, we have to understand how they operate.

We often think of individual figures when we picture angels, but really the angelic mind is a vibration. You can think of it as a force or collective intelligence that is available to us all in any given moment. That mind has four pillars to it, and if you can emulate the energy held in those four pillars, then you can access the angelic vibration. Angelic wisdom, guidance, and support will become easily accessible to you.

It will happen even if you can only tap into one of the pillars. Like attracts like. You can't escape it!

Here are the four pillars:

1. Authenticity

2. Service

3. Devotion

4. Love

Let's start with the first one: authenticity.

Authenticity

Angels are aligned to the highest truth in all circumstances. They aren't about glossing over issues or taking sides. They have a neutral mind (developing one, by the way, is the goal of kundalini yoga). I have found that when people start to live in a more truthful way, the angels are magnetized to them. Through their authenticity, people just start to attract them. I'll give you an example.

Have you ever known someone who is really struggling with their sexuality and finding it difficult to embrace who they are? Perhaps everyone knows this person is gay, but they haven't owned it for themselves. They are shamed from a societal perspective or perhaps because of a religious background. Maybe they are afraid of what their parents will say. Yet when they finally come into themselves, and out to the world, their life starts falling into place.

Authenticity can involve sexuality or any other essential truth. The point is that when people reveal who they are, their style changes and they start making friends easily. There's a spring in their step, there's that radiance. They join the conga line even though they're stone-cold sober, because they're just so damn happy and comfortable in who they are, and it doesn't matter what anyone else thinks. They are effervescent and alive. And you see it on their face.

When someone becomes unapologetically true to themselves, they may get a great job opportunity or some other type of good fortune. That's because the energy of the Universe is coming through to support them.

You might call that energy angels. I do.

◆

Angels are like the Universe's
personal assistants.

So, first we should be aiming for authenticity. It's a great place to start.

Now let's move on to the second pillar.

Service

Angels are all about what they can give, not what they can get. Therefore, when we are in service to others, selfless service, we are emulating them. We should be thinking, *How can I help? How can I offer support? What can I do for someone?*

When we step into the energy of service,
we draw angels toward us.

I was at an event in London once when a woman started waving her hand somewhat frantically. "I have a question," she said, in case the waving hand wasn't a giveaway.

She was a board-certified clinical psychotherapist and not interested in angels in the slightest. So why was she there? One day she had been working on a particularly stubborn case—a man who was suffering from addiction. Feeling desperate in a session with him one day, she had looked down and said to herself, "Please God, help me help this guy. I just want him to get through this."

When she had looked back up at her patient, she had seen a gigantic angel right behind him. The angel told her that the man had become an addict because he wasn't feeling good about his relationship with his father. He had drowned his sorrows in alcohol almost his entire life.

The psychotherapist, remember, wasn't used to consultations with angels. It turned out, however, that she had been interested in the spiritual world for a long time, but worried that it would dilute her clinical expertise if she paid it any mind. Still, a visit from an angel was a bit of a stunner.

At that point she was thinking, *Just what is going on?*, but she relayed the information to the patient, without saying where it had come from. Within a short while, the patient had an incredibly healing experience. So, the psychotherapist's question to me was about why the angel had appeared.

"I've read in every angel book out there that angels don't come unless you invite them," she said. "But I didn't invite them. So why did that one appear?"

I told her that while it was true she hadn't invited an angel through *prayer*, she had attracted one through *service*. Her pure desire to help her patient was what had magnetized the angel to her.

Some people hear about this pillar of angelic connection and feel frustrated because they think it doesn't work for them. "I'm always helping my sister out," they tell me. Or "I do every favor my neighbor asks of me." They often recount their list of obligations with a strained look on their face. They're spending many hours helping other people and yet angels haven't appeared to them.

So, let's go back to the top of this section. Service alone isn't the pillar. It's *selfless* service. It's a pure desire to help. It's not saying "yes" when your heart is saying something else. It's not "My sister is asking me to look after her kids again!" If you're hiding frustration in your heart, that's not service.

Your attitude can draw angels toward you or push them away. Like attracts like. If you're saying "yes" from the heart, not worrying about consequences and time, that kind of energy will attract angels. If you're not, well, would you want your angel rolling their eyes and sighing with frustration behind your back? I didn't think so.

Okay, I think we're ready to move on to the third pillar: devotion.

Devotion

Devotion and service can be the same thing, depending on how they show up, but for this framework I'm going to talk about devotion in terms of honoring the divine.

———————— ♦ ————————

When you light a candle in someone's honor, you
open your home to the presence of angels.

When we praise and give thanks to a higher power, it attracts angels. (It's one of their favorite activities as well.)

During the Covid times, like many other people, I had extra time at home, and I felt called to take up a new hobby to keep myself occupied. I did focus a lot on my work as well, but I've always strongly believed that in order to be a good teacher you have to be a *great* student.

Something that I had wanted to learn ever since my first trip to India in 2013 was how to play harmonium. If you're not familiar with this bulky instrument, it's basically a cross between an organ and an accordion. You play the piano-style keys with your right hand and use your left hand to pump air into the harmonium to power up its organ drone. It sounds very Indian and a little "off-key" to modern ears, but oh my goodness, the sound is gorgeous.

I learned during this odd time for us all that the Grammy-nominated Snatam Kaur, a very well-known devotional singer within the kundalini yoga tradition, had started her own school where you could learn how to play harmonium to accompany chanting and prayers. I immediately signed up and within a short space of time (I think it was around 16 weeks) I was confidently chanting some of my favorite devotional prayers and only a few months later I was able to write my own music for mantras I loved.

Through playing harmonium and developing a daily chanting practice, I strengthened my spiritual connection. Even though I'd been working with angels for almost two decades by then, their presence and messages became clearer than ever.

I'll never forget the first public readings I gave after that time—the clarity of the information that was coming through made even my own hair stand on end.

♦ ♦ ♦

Devotion is when we give ourselves fully without needing to receive, when we're not looking for anything in return. I've seen incredible examples of it at Hindu temples, among Hare Krishna chanters, and in households of Islamic royalty. It doesn't matter who you are or where you're from—the kind of devotion I'm talking about can happen anywhere.

One time in India I went to the famous Arunachalesvara temple. The streetlights were terrible and it was super dark, even though I think there was a full moon that night. People were on their knees in front of an altar, all praising the name of the divine. I've never seen as many angels in my life as I did at that temple that night.

Another time I went to the Middle East to work with a few members of an Arabic royal family. I was heading to the house of a princess in the royal compound. As soon as I walked into her hallway, I was greeted by angels. In the background I heard Islamic music playing quietly.

"There are so many angels here!" I told the princess, who explained that she played prayers in her home all day and all night on a loop. She had been told by a priest that it would keep away evil, and I genuinely believe it would.

All day long, all night long, those prayers played. And the angels came.

Of course they came. Angels are just *waiting* for us to for us to step into devotion. They're on standby. In a constant state of praise. When we join them, we'll feel them all around us.

And now it's time for the last pillar: love.

Love

Love. Here we go again! It's always about love. (Insert one of my oldest friends, maybe Robyn, giving me a playful eye roll.)

The kind of love I'm talking about is beyond comprehension. I think the best way to describe it is when you tell someone your deepest darkest secret and they love you anyway. *Unconditional* love.

I think that's why Louise Hay was so spiritually connected. One of my favorite Louise Hay stories is when she opened her living room to men with AIDS back before it was known how it spread. Louise had already been doing the Science of Mind events, talking about the power of mind over matter. After one event a man approached her and said he wanted to talk about AIDS. "I'm scared," he told her. "Actually there are a few of us and we're really, really scared."

"Come to my house," said Louise, "and we'll do what I've always known to work. We'll just love ourselves anyway."

So, they showed up at her door, these guys who were really suffering. Most had struggled with their sexuality, and now they might have had this horrific disease that no one really understood. And Louise took them in, and she kissed them and cuddled them. That's angelic love. It doesn't matter what we've done or how scared we are or how many people are scared of *us*, angels love us anyway. If only we could love ourselves that much, how much brighter might our paths become.

———————————— ♦ ————————————

To love someone wholly and fully
is to embody angelic love.

Experiencing Angels

Experiencing angels is about connecting to divine love. We call that love different names. Perhaps we call it God. We may call it Source, or the Universe, or something else. Whatever you call it, for me, it's all the same thing. The names don't really matter. What we're after is a feeling.

It's a feeling of love, an expression of light, and a sense of being protected. A feeling of knowing you're surrounded by forces that want the best for you. A sense of peace. It's not something we have to chase, rather something that will come to us when we pull back from forcing things to happen. It's a kind of ease. It's always there in the here and now, waiting for us to arrive or what I like to call "lean in."

I know you can have this feeling and this protection, and that's why I'm so committed to this cause. There's no doubt in my mind that you can experience angels and have your prayers answered. What about you? One of the reasons people sometimes have trouble experiencing angels is they don't really believe that they can.

In the second chapter we talked a bit about why you shouldn't be afraid to experience angels, as it really just means experiencing love. Now, I know reading one chapter telling you not to be afraid doesn't mean you won't be. But I do believe in miracles, and I believe in what I learned from *A Course in Miracles*, which is that a miracle is a shift in perception. It's that moment you are willing to think differently about something—the moment you choose between feeling fear or accepting love. From angels, perhaps.

Speaking about this topic takes me back to a breakthrough moment that happened in Canada. I was there with my publisher, Hay House, speaking at an event called "Mystical Connections" in Toronto. It's an amazing gathering that brings some of the best psychics, mediums, healers, and intuitives together in one space. All of them share their version of spirituality, and of course I was speaking about angels. I was the youngest of all the speakers, and although I love hanging out with my colleagues, some of whom happen to be my childhood spiritual heroes, the energy of the room felt a little flat. So, before going on stage, I asked the sound guy if I could plug in my laptop to play music.

As soon as I got on stage in front of maybe 900 people, I asked, "Who's in the mood for a dance?" Fleetwood Mac's "Go Your Own Way" came on full blast and before you knew it, everyone was up dancing, jumping, and laughing with their friends, strangers, and a bunch of psychics.

When the song ended and we caught our breath, I launched into my presentation. It went really well and afterward during the book-signing I had the most beautiful heart-to-heart with a local woman. It was only a brief interaction, but long enough for a couple things to click into place for me with my work.

"I really enjoyed your presentation today," she told me.

I thanked her. "That really means a lot!" I reached out to take the copy of *Angel Prayers* she was holding in her hand. "What's your name?"

"It's Cheryl," she said with a smile.

As I started to write a short line in Cheryl's book and sign it for her, she leaned in a little closer and spoke quietly.

"I'll be honest, until I heard you speak today, your presentation was the one I was looking forward to the least. Please don't take this wrong, but I've always been somewhat repulsed by the idea of angels. Your presentation completely changed that for me and now I'm really open to the idea."

"Repulsed? That's a really strong reaction to angels!"

"I know. I've never been able to understand it myself. Why did I feel like that until just now?"

Before I could even think about what to say next, I was already saying it. "Because you weren't ready for that love."

I could see the wheels turning in Cheryl's mind. Then I got a psychic hit that she'd been working hard on her own self-healing.

"All of the inner work you have been doing," I continued, "has led you to this point. For so long you felt unworthy and not good enough. That was the barricade that kept love away. And now, here you are, someone who has done a deep dive into your own self-healing, your own self-respect, and you are arriving at a place that can only be described as self-love. That's why you're now ready to welcome in angels!"

Cheryl gasped, and before I knew it, she was in my arms crying.

I knew as I held her that Cheryl's miracle wasn't just her shift in perception about angels and her openness to their love, it was the fact that in some weird and wonderful way she was now able to consider that this kind of healing was possible for *her*.

You being here now, reading this book—even if it's just out of curiosity— means there's a part of you, too, that has reached a knowing that divine love is possible and available to you, and for me, that's thrilling!

·8·

Attracting Angels

"Angel of God,
My guardian dear,
to whom God's love commits me here,
ever this day be at my side, to light
and guard, to rule and guide.
Amen."

"Guardian Angel Prayer"
from Reginald's Life of St. Malchus[1]

In this chapter I want to talk about how to make encounters with angels more likely. If you've read my book *Raise Your Vibration*, you may already know quite a bit about some of the practices like gratitude, affirmative prayer, manifestation, visualization, lighting candles, surrounding yourself in golden light, cutting cords of fear, and dispelling negative energy.

——————————— ♦ ———————————

Visualizing yourself immersed in golden
light allows you to attract angels.

———————————————————————

For now, I want to debunk some myths about angels that might be hindering your ability to invite them into your life. Twenty years into my work with angels, I realize I need to break down some of the old constructs that aren't serving us anymore. I've come to understand that some of the accepted knowledge about angels has created roadblocks for people. So I want to help you lose any preconceived ideas you may have that are interfering with your experience of angels. My hope is this shift will lead to a more authentic connection.

When I was first exposed to this world, I felt I had to adapt to the angel experts' vision of things. Don't get me wrong, I'm super grateful for the trailblazers that paved the way, but at the same time they set up standards that sometimes felt a bit rigid and dogmatic. When we had a difference of opinion and mine wasn't well accepted, I ended up glossing over it to make things easier. I remember getting back the marked-up manuscript for my first book and the editor had flagged places where what I had said contradicted the accepted knowledge about angels. For example, I saw Gabriel as a fierce African warrior, while a famous expert saw her with red hair. I was also focused on the fact that Mary was an ordinary girl. Others thought she was an embodiment of the goddess Isis who had come here knowing what she was supposed to do in this lifetime.

In workshops and conferences, I also faced pushback when my ideas weren't in line with those of the dominant angel experts. In Germany especially, I remember people really getting upset about some of my ideas.

At one workshop a broad-shouldered woman stood up in front of the room and said bluntly, "You're wrong! This is wrong!"

She proceeded to argue that we couldn't have more than one angel.

I asked her why she felt that way. We went back and forth. Through an interpreter!

I talked a bit about how in Islam you have one guardian angel on your left and one on your right, one recording all the good you are doing, the other recording the bad. In the Bible, when Mary of Magdala arrived at the tomb of Christ, there were two angels, one where his head had lain and the other where his feet had been. For me, both of those accounts are saying there are angels everywhere and all of them want to help us. So, who are we to say you're only allowed to have one angel?

The woman wasn't having it, but I didn't need to prove that I was right, I was more interested in finding out why she was so set on the rules. I tried to stay in the inquiry of it all.

But for me, angels are love, and love has no bounds. It is beyond confinement.

The way I see it, getting to know angels isn't like dogmatic religion, it's personal spirituality. I think spiritual texts and religion help us get to grips with spiritual ideas, but we shouldn't be limited by what's written. Gosh! Can you imagine someone from biblical times seeing us do a Facetime call? It would be branded as witchcraft, and that in itself says a lot about limitations. For me, religion is what someone tells you about the divine, and spirituality is having your own experience of it. There's a vast difference between the two.

Loosening Up

So, as well as dropping the rules, I think we should maybe loosen up a little in our approach to angels. They will become more approachable to us when we become more approachable to them. That means getting away from scarcity thinking, which only makes us stiff and unable to receive all the love that is out there.

In my book *Angel Prayers*, I wrote about how angels liked to have fun and how I'd even seen them dancing sometimes back when I was a DJ. One reader thought I meant I'd seen angels doing Top Rock or some other current dance moves. We had a bit of a laugh about that, as I clarified that I'd seen their light swirling around the dance floor, not angelic figures getting down. (I couldn't help but demonstrate what the angels *weren't* doing, which made the situation all the more ludicrous.) So, while I'm debunking myths about angels, I don't want to go too far in the other direction. They're not out there throwing back vodka shots at a superclub in Ibiza. But they're not buttoned-up schoolmarms either. They're *not* wagging their fingers and telling everyone, "You can only have one of us and you've reached your limit!"

Angels are limitless. Keeping this in mind will
lead to more rewarding angel experiences.

I'd like to talk about three specific areas where I think people can stumble: trying to see an angel, trying to find out an angel's name, and worrying about whether they can talk directly to an angel.

We'll take them one by one.

"Why can't I see my angel?"

People come up to me in book-signing lines all the time and hit me with some version of "I just can't see my angel. I don't know what's wrong."

It's quite clear many of these people are getting really frustrated. Some tell me their failure is testing their faith. They want to believe, but sometimes they're not sure they do anymore.

Some people think they aren't seeing angels because they haven't raised their vibration high enough. That kind of thinking only spirals into more anxiety, though, and takes us further away from the frequency where angels like to hang out.

I know where these people are coming from. Back when I started, I just accepted that seeing angels was the goal. Everyone was desperate to see an angel and come back with a description of the eye and hair color. Everyone was desperate to hear about it. "Were there wings?" "What color was their aura?" "Were there sparkles?" "How was he dressed?" "Did he carry a sword?"

People used to argue about Archangel Michael. "He's got blond hair and blue eyes." "No, he's got brown hair and blue eyes!" When I had the chance to create an oracle deck, I made him Black. But we don't know what he looks like. We're trying to make something that is unbounded energy—God, Source, the Universe—into something flat and finite, something we can see with our limited vision. That's not getting us anywhere. That's reducing angels to fit the constraints of our sensory abilities, when they're so much bigger than that.

And what if we stop worrying about seeing angels altogether? What if seeing isn't the point anyway?

Remember at the start of this chapter I said we're after a feeling?

———————— ◆ ————————

Feeling the presence of an angel is way
more important than seeing one.

————————————————————

What if we focused on *feeling* the angels around us rather than trying to see them?

Let our goal be accessing the feeling, the visceral not the visual. Sentience—that's where all the magic is! It's the inner world we need to pay attention to, not the outer. If you watch any great medium or psychic, when they start getting the real stuff, they close their eyes.

So, if you are desperate to see your angel and feel your faith is being tested, I hope you can start to understand that angels are all around you whether you can see them or not. The point is to become quiet enough to sit peacefully alongside these gentle creatures and become aware of their presence.

When I understood that our focus had to shift away from angel observation, almost like bird-watching—*I spotted one!*—to the idea that we want to exist on a plane with angel energy, it really started to unlock things for me. We can help make that angelic connection. We have so much more power than we realize.

It's kind of like a play on Gandhi's famous line about being "the change you want to see." If you want to experience angels, you have to be more like them.

I started to teach that way of approaching angels instead. And I found that that's when we get to experience their essence—their unconditional love, their limitless capacity to forgive, their steadfast support.

I was about to walk out of my office building in Glasgow one day when a woman stopped me in the hall. She, was wearing a light gray rain jacket and had a little leather handbag hanging from the crook of her arm.

"I was hoping to catch you," she said, peering up at me through little round gold-colored glasses.

I gave her my number so she could make an appointment.

She shook her head. "I need to speak with you today. Can you make an exception?"

It turned out she was in a really scary place with her health. She had cancer and wanted to know if she was going to get through it and be okay.

I told her I wasn't a healer, but she said she just wanted to say a prayer with me.

So I closed my eyes and asked her to imagine a golden light around her. "Take two deep breaths," I told her, taking a few deep breaths myself.

I had hardly started the prayer when she told me she could see two angels, one on either side of her.

I asked, "How do you feel your angels see you?"

"They can see me as healed!" she said with a calm kind of wonder in her voice. "The angels can see me as healed," she said again. "They don't see me sick. They see me perfect, whole, and healed."

Those words almost sounded channeled. *Perfect, whole, and healed.*

Several months later I received a card with a daffodil on the front.

"You may not remember me," the woman from the hallway had written. "I showed up at your office and asked you to say a prayer for me, and that really touched me."

Of course I remembered.

"I want to tell you that I have gone into remission."

I was so pleased to hear that. The experience had touched me as well. In fact, I started to use her phrase in my work. *Perfect, whole, and healed.* What a beautiful way to be seen.

So, let's go beyond the idea of seeing angels and embody how we want to be seen. How do you think your angels see you? How would you like them to see you? How can you be more like what you'd like them to see?

What's in a name?

Okay, now we're ready to go back to the book-signing line again. Another common refrain here is about not being able to find out the name of an angel. One woman told me, "I've been trying to find out my guardian angel's name for twenty-five years. I've tried every meditation from every angel expert, and nothing is coming through."

Well, this kind of goes back to the point I was making earlier about different names for the same idea—love. We can call it God or something else.

———————————— ♦ ————————————

**Names are just signifiers in our language.
The energy is what matters.**

———————————————————————————

So, you might get a name for your angel. It's kind of fun if you do. But you needn't get a name.

Let me tell you about an experience where what a woman saw was so much more powerful than a random name might have been. It was at an event I used to host monthly called Angel Club. We originally started meeting at a place called Tir Na nOg, which means "Land of Youth" in Gaelic. It's a spiritual center that was converted from old stables in Balfron, a little town tucked in the hills between Glasgow and Loch Lomond. I would give an inspirational talk on angels, lead a meditation, take questions, and then do mini-readings at the end. Everyone would get an angel card on their chair to take home. I hosted it for about eight years, beginning in my mid-twenties.

That particular night I led the group with a visualization into a super-centered state. First we imagined ourselves protected by a golden light and then we saw ourselves on a beach in front of a sparkling cave covered with amethysts. Inside the cave was a bench, and each of us had a guardian angel waiting on the bench for us.

When we came out of the visualization, one woman shared her experience. She had seen a blue triangle hovering over the bench. That might sound strange, but to her it felt exactly right. The triangle was shimmering with protective energy, and she felt safe. It turned out she was wearing a blue triangle pendant around her neck and had an attachment to that particular symbol. Her angel manifested in that form at that time to her because it was comforting and familiar to her. If she had been looking for a person to appear, intent on noting her outfit or the color of her hair, she might have missed her triangle angel entirely!

And she didn't need a name. The feeling was everything.

You don't need a name. When you are in the presence of something awe-inspiring in nature, you might gasp and call it incredible or sublime, but you don't need a name for what you feel, do you? If you didn't know the words "awe," or "wonder," or "astonishment," or "beauty," or anything else to describe a dazzling sunset or a magnificent glacial lake, wouldn't you still *feel* the same way in its presence?

Angels are energy and vibration.

You don't need to call your angel's name to summon them, you need to bring yourself into the right energy and vibration. A name won't make your connection with your angel any stronger. And an overzealous focus on finding a name might distract from the opportunity just to revel in the strength and protection your angel is ready to provide for you.

Speaking directly to angels

There is another shift I want to address—praying directly to angels. In more traditional religious spaces, it's often frowned upon to speak directly to any higher powers. That is a practice reserved for priests, pastors, rabbis, and other higher-ups. (Starting to feel that stiff, buttoned-up feeling again.) But let's pause for a second and think about why the people in charge might not want us to have direct access to higher powers. Wouldn't that undermine their role a bit? If we can speak directly to an angel, then maybe we don't need the intermediary. We're going to become less dependent on the connection the priest or pastor or rabbi has, right? That doesn't mean we need to reject their wisdom. I believe we can have our own direct connection with angels and learn from others as well. But anyone who tries to cut off our direct connection may not have our best interest at heart. It may be more about filling the pews and keeping a congregation.

There is room enough for all of us, and room enough for all of us to experience angels all the time. They're not a limited resource.

I actually got a letter from a priest at the Vatican not long ago saying that he appreciated what I had to say about angels and especially the idea of thanking them. In Catholicism, as I mentioned earlier, you're allowed to speak to angels directly. For Baptists, the emphasis tends to be on not having direct communication. Different traditions have different approaches, and of course things are changing all the time. As of the past half-century, women can become rabbis, a reform that surely would have surprised Mary of Nazareth.

What I want you to know is that you can speak directly to angels. You are worthy of that conversation. We all are. You have access to their insight and protection at all times. You don't have to see them clearly. You may see an image or may get more of a feeling. You don't have to know the name of the angel whose voice you hear. You do have to know angels are all around you. They're there for you.

If you aren't feeling satisfied with your connection with angels, it's important to remember they are energy, and to stop and think about what energy you are giving off at the moment. Like attracts like, and it's never truer than when we're talking about these peaceful, timeless beings.

The purest part of your soul, I think, has already connected with your angel, whether you have recognized the experience or not. In fact, I believe we connect with our angels before we come into this world, whether we have lived a previous life or not. That's one reason why a sense of familiarity often washes over us when we experience our angels. I like to think of it as a remembering. Embracing the world of angels might sometimes feel like you're entering a strange new place, but it's a place of holiness and wholeness that may feel quite familiar. Maybe almost like home.

For me, God is beyond religion, and angels, as messengers of God, are beyond religion as well. These beings are older and wiser than the linear systems we have.

Now some people wonder why we would want to communicate with angels rather than with God directly. That does have a very simple answer: angels are "of God."

—————————— ♦ ——————————

When we're communicating with angels,
we're communicating with God.

—————————————————————

It's a pretty big claim, right, to say that we're communicating with God. But I believe that's what we're doing here. Of course I'm just a boy from Greenock, Scotland, who has always kind of existed in between two worlds. A boy who saw his grandmother after she died. A teen who was given an angel card deck. A man who has had a bizarre number of metaphysical experiences.

I'm sharing everything I've learned, but I also want to let you know that I'm still searching. I'm still on a path of discovery. I don't have all the answers and I'm not going to pretend that I do. I will never understand why children die. And I certainly don't like to say that things happen for a reason or that things will always work out for the best. I honestly don't know. I really don't. How can we say that at the same time as we watch images of children covered in blood running from bombs? *That's their childhood*, I think to myself, with a sob in my throat. I can't cope. I can't deal with it. *That's their childhood.*

And those are the ones still alive. When I look in the eyes of a parent who has lost a child, I'm not going to tell them it happened for a reason or that God called that child home. It does sometimes cross my mind that maybe there are souls that are too pure for the harshness of this world. But I can't say I know for sure.

I like to advise people who are looking for answers to go inside themselves rather than look outward for an article, a book, or an authority. This kind of searching requires quiet. And it's a kind of searching that has been valued in spiritual communities for millennia. Perhaps you know the story of how the Buddha wouldn't respond to people asking questions, rather giving them silence in which they could contemplate and perhaps find their own answers.

Or maybe you've heard of Abraham Joshua Heschel. He was a Polish-American rabbi who was a prominent figure in the American civil rights movement. (In fact, you may have seen him in several iconic photographs next to Dr. Martin Luther King Jr. crossing the Edmund Pettus Bridge in Selma, Alabama, and protesting the Vietnam War.) I don't know if Abraham and I would have all that much in common in terms of our spiritual beliefs, although he wrote a book about the Sabbath which indicates that the value we place on sacred time and ritual would certainly overlap. His daughter, Susannah Heschel, is the head of Jewish studies at Dartmouth University in New Hampshire. When asked to talk about her father's faith, she said, "A religious person is always questioning, challenging, never satisfied."[2]

I am always questioning. I'm pretty comfortable challenging established beliefs. Never satisfied? Depends on how you define the word.

I don't have the answers for why one child gets to live a life of playing football and laughing with friends while another is running from gunfire, not sure if he'll ever see his family again. I don't have those answers, but I'm open. I'm open to answers and always open to the unfolding possibility for grace. And that grace can be more awareness of things seen and unseen. That's my career. I deal in the unseen. Often the unnamed. Many times the just-out-of-reach.

◆ ◆ ◆

It isn't necessary to engage with the worst horrors on the planet to consider the idea of whether or not things happen for a reason. Usually one that's not obvious at the time.

When I was in school, my guidance teacher asked what I wanted to be when I grew up. I said I wanted to be a Hay House author. Really!

"What's Hay House?" she asked.

I told her it was a publisher that specialized in spiritual authors and teachers.

Well, she told me, if I wanted to be an author, I would need to go to university and probably need an English degree.

I had been a bit of a class clown in school. I was always a bit distracted. And I always had an opinion. About everything. That got me into plenty of run-ins with teachers.

But after reading books by Louise Hay, I knew I wanted to make something of my life. So I set my mind to working to go to university. I was determined to get my grades up and get my focus down. And it worked. Soon I was doing really well in English and exceptionally well in Religious Studies.

I started to scout universities. Here in the UK you do it a year or two before you leave school, deciding on which university you want to apply to and which subject you want to study. Then your school supports you in the studies that will get you there. So, I was applying myself to Religious Studies and planning on studying that at a certain university. Only when it came time the following autumn to enroll in the school course that would get me there, I was the only person in my year to apply. So, the school decided they wouldn't run the course. Instead of suggesting that I attend another school for that subject, or figuring out some other way of supporting me, they just didn't run the course. I ended up having to do Politics instead.

I was deflated, but I muddled through most of the year.

Then one day in maths class, some kids were being silly in the back of the classroom. The teacher, Miss Carmichael, was getting really frustrated, and finally she burst out, "I've had enough of this class!"

I was like, "Guys, come on. It's our last class before the final exams. Let her get us to where we need to be."

"I'm not teaching this class anymore!" Miss Carmichael said, slamming her workbook down on the front table.

The rest of the class started to giggle. They had won!

I knew this wasn't going to be good. I said, "Miss Carmichael, can we please, please continue with the lesson?"

"That's what I was *trying* to do!" she huffed back.

I don't know how, but finally everyone was quiet, ready to continue.

But she wasn't. "You're all hopeless! You're all a bunch of idiots!"

"Now you're just trying to bicker," I told her.

"If you don't like what I'm saying, Kyle, you can leave this class right now and never come back to this school."

I was the youngest in my year. I was just old enough legally to leave school. And that's what I did. I walked out. I never went back. They failed me so badly, that school. They so let me down! I was *so* ready for Religious Studies, and they wouldn't run it.

And yet here I am writing my ninth book about angels and spirituality. I know I've been so blessed to connect with so many people—and so many angels—and to do my tiny part to bring these realms closer together. Can I say for sure that I am in a better position now because the adults around me didn't figure out a way for me to pursue that dream I had when I was young? I don't know what my path would have been had I stayed there and been able to take that Religious Studies course. If I'd studied Religion at university, would I know more than I know now? Would I be more satisfied?

I've followed the path that unfolded before me, but I've had doubts along the way. You know there was a time when I put away my cards and my crystals and threw myself into DJing. I've worked at an airport and a hotel. I've wondered at times, even last week, *Is this to be my life? Is this the life that I want?* Perhaps I am someone who will always be questioning.

But that means I'm always open to new truths and new understandings. Seeking to understand the mystery. The great mystery.

One way to discover more is, of course, to speak to angels.

·9·

Speaking to Angels

"O, speak again, bright angel, for thou art
As glorious to this night, being o'er my head,
As is a wingèd messenger of heaven
Unto the white upturnèd wond'ring eyes
Of mortals that fall back to gaze on him
When he bestrides the lazy puffing clouds
And sails upon the bosom of the air."

WILLIAM SHAKESPEARE, *ROMEO AND JULIET*

In the 20 years of my inquiry into angels I've found that most people feel the need to connect with these phenomenal beings during a time of change. Often it's because something has shifted in their life—maybe there's been a sudden loss or a challenge that has been beyond their control. Maybe they're in a space of overwhelm or indecision. Whatever the reason, something magical is happening. Skeptics might say that they're just looking for something to fill a void, but I believe something miraculous is occurring.

In moments of darkness, angels draw close. In truth, they are always there, waiting for us to become aware of their presence. But when we're thrown into darkness, their light becomes more apparent—it's as if our soul can feel it and knows that we're not alone and that something "out there" can help us.

Our heart is a walkie-talkie to angels;
they hear the prayers we whisper within.

Are you looking for help now? Is that why you picked up this book?

But another question is: Are you calling out to angels or are angels calling out to you? Are you looking for a closer connection with them or still hesitating?

Remember that having direct communication with an angel means you are coming into your own power. Some of us aren't sure we want all that power. Perhaps you've heard the famous Marianne Williamson quote: "Our deepest fear is not that we are inadequate. Our deepest fear is that we are powerful beyond measure."[1]

Part of you isn't sure how powerful you want to be, right? You may have dreamed of the spotlight for years, but how will it feel when you're center-stage and it's pointed right at you? When the room is packed with people waiting to hear what you have to say? Maybe for a moment you'll wish you had stood in the back, stayed part of the chorus, and let someone else take the lead.

But, since angels are here to empower you, conversations with angels are about your evolution—about embracing a process of renewal, letting go of the past, and moving into the future.

The moment you're willing to face your fear and have that conversation is the moment you embrace your own power. It's the moment you start bringing all the light you were meant to bring to this world.

Shifting Energy

I often talk about how we need to raise our vibration to communicate with angels. It might sound like a lot of work, but I promise you it's really the opposite. It's cleansing, healing, and will lighten your life in multiple ways. It's letting go of energy that's not serving you. It's cutting out draining thoughts and draining situations. Once you immerse yourself in raising your vibration, whether it's getting on the meditation mat or getting outside to hear the birds, it won't feel like work at all. Raising your vibration is empowering.

When we're raising our vibration, we're not passively hoping an angel will approach us, like a shy middle-school kid at a school dance, hoping someone will ask him to join in the Macarena. Instead we're consistently practicing techniques that help us get closer to where angels hang out.

Let me talk a little bit about vibration just in terms of human spaces. I want to show you some examples of raising the vibration in these everyday spaces, because it can help us make the leap to thinking about the spiritual realm.

Do you ever walk into a room and know the vibe is just *off*? Perhaps your body suddenly feels tense. People's faces look drawn. No one's smiling. There's a heavy mood. It's like that in a pharmacy where I pick up my mum's medicine. There's a dense vibe because the staff are completely stretched meeting the needs of the public. It creates anxiety in everyone approaching the counter.

So, what I do is I go in and intentionally change the energy. I go out of my way to ask whoever is serving me how they are and say hi to anyone else who's working there if they catch my eye or pass the front desk.

I learned to shift energy like this when I was in a corporate job around the age of 20. I was working at a hotel as an event organizer and the rest of the staff had all been there for at least a decade. When I came in as this new kid on the block, using the internet to create new ideas and business, I was met with resistance. But I received a message from the angels about how to change the energy in my workplace: "Whatever is missing is your job to bring."

—————— ♦ ——————

Whatever is missing is your job to bring.

So I brought it. I showed up with love and joy in my heart every day and I shared my love of all things angels with the team. On my final day at that position, when I was moving on to become a full-time angel guy, every senior staff member had their angel card of the day on their desk and affirmations all around their computer screens! The energy had just been contagious.

I have the best shot at entering a space and lifting it up if I've done the work to raise my own vibration first, so staying faithful to my routine really helps. For example, did I make time for prayer (beginning with thanking angels) today? Did I take time to acknowledge my connection to everything in the Universe? Did I embrace the day as a co-creator of my experiences? Did I meditate? Set intentions? Have I got on my yoga mat? Am I choosing to stay present?

If I can walk in knowing I'm being held by angels, then I can surely hold space for the people who are having a tough day. After all, I know I'm not the only one lifting them up!

There's another place where I've gone about intentionally shifting energy—my neighborhood. My house was the first built on the street. My five-pound chihuahua, Thor, and I were the first to move in. As people started to join the neighborhood, it was weird to me that they weren't waving to one another. I always made an effort to say hello and wave, and most people embraced that friendliness. And now people do wave to me first, and I see them greeting one another as well.

I like to think of changing the energy as infiltration in a positive way. You change it from the inside, by becoming part of the scene and then moving the vibe in a different direction. With angels at your side, of course!

Let's take this idea and apply it to the angel world.

Angels are always joyful and connected. So, guess what works best for us when we want to speak with them? You guessed it.

———————— ♦ ————————

Before we even start talking to angels, we can put ourselves in a position to align with their energy.

———————————————————

What helps you feel connected to angels? How about feeling joyful? Grateful? Glowing? What are some of the ways you like to center yourself and raise your vibe?

This doesn't have to happen immediately, especially if the idea is new to you. Angels want you to go at your own pace and trust in divine timing. Angels always send an answer, but with divine timing.

Allow yourself to be supported along this path. Start small. Why not start with this?

> Take three deep breaths.
>
> Set an intention for the day.
>
> Imagine yourself surrounded in golden light.
>
> Invite the Universe in.
>
> Choose to embrace and honor your power.
>
> Say this simple prayer:
>
> > *Thank you, angels, for reminding me of your presence. It feels so good to know you are here.*
>
> Take a deep breath. Sigh it out.
>
> Become aware of any sensations you feel.
>
> Be open to thoughts of inspiration, love, and forgiveness.
>
> If it feels good to you, close your eyes.
>
> Move into the knowing that you are surrounded by a presence of love.
>
> If you feel in some way that you are not alone, take in all of the impressions.
>
> Can you feel it with your body? If so, is the presence on your left or right, in front or behind?
>
> Can you see any colors in your mind? If not, ask to see one.
>
> Can you smell anything?

Do you feel warm or cool?

Ask yourself this question: "If I was my angel, knowing that they are a being of love, what do I feel they would want me to know?"

Whatever you receive is your angel's message for you.

All the impressions that you have received are the tools you can use to build up the intuitive ability to know when angels are near.

To close your practice, say, "Thank you, angels!"

If you closed your eyes, open them.

Stretch, smile, and continue on.

If you have the time, perhaps you can take a little walk in nature or take 10 minutes to meditate.

If you ever need to feel your angel's love, get out in nature and invite them to be close to you. A conversation with angels doesn't have to be the kind of conversation we have with a friend or loved one, although it may be. Angels are infinite beings, so they have infinite ways of interacting with us.

Take a moment to check in with yourself.

How do you feel now compared to when you started reading this chapter? Has your energy changed at all?

What is being revealed to you?

Take some time for reflection.

Now let's turn our attention for a bit to the idea of speaking to angels. After all, that's the title of the chapter.

Give and Take

How *do* we speak to angels? Well, a lot of people approach God like they're showing up to Costco. *I'll take this. I'll grab one of those. Oh yeah, I need a refill of these things over here.* Sadly, I often see a lot of that kind of behavior in manifestation circles. *I want.* So much *I want!* It's a fever of goal-setting.

———— ♦ ————

Approaching God like you're in a giant warehouse
shop or he's a genie—neither one is ideal.

Angels *can* bring you things you want and grant wishes. There does come a point in everyone's spiritual journey when they first get connected and a lot of their wishes are granted. It's a sparkly demonstration that something is happening. Something is out there. A big part of that energy is our enthusiasm—we're feeling connected and buzzing. We're part of something bigger!

But I have to warn you if your wishes become overly materialistic, the angels will stop granting them, because, after all, they're *not* the genie from *Aladdin*.

It's also possible that the reverse happens. Some of us start out super committed to meaning and purpose. We're drawn to angels to make a difference in our lives and the lives of everyone we know. We want to create a sense of healing and connectedness. But somewhere along the way we get sucked into treating angels like our virtual assistants, and this isn't going to support our spiritual growth and expansion.

I remember asking for a Mini Cooper when I was younger. I asked for other things as well. (Yes, you might call it a kind of "shopping list.") I would ask the angels to make all the traffic lights green when I was running late, or for enough cash to pay my bills, and I even asked them to help me get promotional deals when I first became an author.

As I became more and more connected to angels, though, I started to ask for *feelings*. When I wanted a thing, I would ask myself, *What does that thing represent?* Maybe the Mini Cooper represented freedom, independence, a sense of not being held back. So, my approach shifted. I would thank the angels for showing me how I could step into a new sense of freedom, for example. I would ask for guidance about how I could use my independence better.

And what's kind of weird is that asking for feelings ended up leading to things I wanted but hadn't asked for. What I learned was if I could be more focused on feeling certain ways, everything I needed, and more, would be given to me anyway.

I used to think maybe the intense wish-granting slowed down because for the angels the novelty had worn off. I could picture them rolling their eyes a bit. "Here he comes, asking for another check to clear his overdrawn bank account." But now I think I understand that it's not that the angels are getting annoyed with us—it's okay to show up with wants and needs—but once we have had a demonstration that miracles are possible, in order for us to level up or live with more meaning, we have to get out of the needy mindset. If we don't grow out of it, we'll never grow, and that's what angels want for us more than anything.

If you go back to the real reason you were called to angels, it was a call for evolution. So, an angel supporting you might hear your shopping list and think, *I have to hold back now, because you're not evolving. If I instantly give you everything on your list, you won't grow.*

Angels are here to give you all you need
rather than all you want.

So the angel stops giving you everything you're asking for. Just like a parent who knows that receiving a million new toys won't make their child any more fulfilled in life. Sometimes our prayers not being answered *is* the answer.

Our relationship may need to become more balanced, too. Think about a friend who always shows up when he needs something. Have you ever had one of those? You don't hear from him for months and then, sure enough, he pings you, asking for a favor. Maybe he needs you to walk his dog or write a review for his business. Or he's looking for a place to crash for the weekend. Or maybe it's not a favor exactly, but he still wants something from you—he'd like you to come to his comedy show next Saturday.

How does that make you feel? Let's be real: *it sucks!* We all know how sucky that kind of friendship is. So don't be that kind of friend to your angels. Don't only show up when you're hoping to get good results on a blood test or a job promotion. The relationship can't be take, take, take. It also has to be: "What can I give? How can I show up? What can I contribute? How can I serve?"

---— ◆ ———

Ask yourself this: "If I was an angel, what would I want myself to know?"

The answer is their answer.

We've all heard of rich people who "have everything," but seem dissatisfied in life. And some of the happiest people I've come across have been those who have had very little, materially speaking. What they have had is a wealth of meaning and purpose. All they've wanted in life is peace for all beings.

Now don't get me wrong. I love material things. I've got a Jeep Wrangler. I love driving it. Every time I start the engine, I feel so cool. I can't help smiling to myself as I'm driving along. I love trucks and boy toys and all kinds of stuff—sneakers anyone? I've met people who have renounced worldly things, but I haven't done it myself. However, I have learned some things about what matters, including that I can't base my happiness on those things, and, as I mentioned earlier, what angels really want for us is spiritual expansion.

Let's review some of the points we've discussed so far about speaking to them:

- When you raise your vibration, you attract angels. Like a magnet.

- If you want to connect to angels, be like them. Embody their peaceful energy.

- You can ask angels for material things, but don't approach them with a shopping list.

- Focus on asking for feelings more than things.

- Be a friend to angels. Don't show up only when you want something.

- Angels aren't there to satisfy your every wish or whim, but to help you evolve.

Now we're going to get even more specific about how we speak to angels, starting with how to *start* speaking to them.

Thanking Angels

It may seem counterintuitive to start with this—don't you get the thing you asked for and *then* offer a thank-you?—but thanking angels is one of the most important ways of communicating with them. It's an opportunity to thank these divine beings for helping line up all the blessings of our day, and these aren't just the moments when we have giant answers to our prayers, they're the ones that we can take for granted. I'll give you an example. Say you treat a friend to coffee and they say, "Thank you." I always say, "Thank you, angels!" when that happens.

Thanking angels is about getting into that magnetic energy of being grateful for all of the blessings in life, big and small. When we are grateful, we create a golden aura, and this golden energy makes us radiant and draws angels in, along with more blessings. So, the more we are grateful, the more we have to be grateful for. Gratitude makes us magnetic to the blessings of angels.

Now, if you have a religious background, you may be concerned about thanking angels rather than thanking God. Sometimes people are worried about this. But, if you remember, I explained earlier that though they may seem to be individual beings, angels are part of the One, part of the whole. They are the heartbeats of God, and when you thank them, you are also thanking the heart of God! There is no separation.

So, the more you model yourself on angels, the more kindness and peace you bring to the world. And nothing could make them happier.

Not only that, but I've found that when I'm in an authentic gratitude vibration with my angels, they're working to let everything in my life work out for me. I get a *knowing* that all I need and more is going to be given to me.

This isn't: *You've given me this—thank you! Now you've given me this—thanks for that as well!* That's far too transactional. Instead, it's a reciprocal giving relationship. That's what you want to enter into with your angels.

———————————— ♦ ————————————

Angels don't want to hear us thanking them
because they want the glory or to be worshipped.
They love to hear us thanking them because our
genuine gratitude magnetizes miracles to us.

————————————————————————

I started thanking angels as a way of opening a conversation with them, and now a lot of other people are doing this as well. To begin with, it felt as if I was taking a stand against what others were teaching. First, people were scared to give angels glory and not God. I hope I've already explained why this needn't be a concern. Second, I've noticed that, particularly with Brits, thanking as if what you're asking for has already been delivered is considered a little forward, perhaps a bit presumptuous. But in fact it removes us from the transactional and takes us into the realm of gratitude and a feedback loop of reciprocity instead.

Now this practice is becoming more mainstream. Try it. It feels really good to open a conversation with a thank-you. It's a little bit like beginning our day with gratitude. *What can I already be thankful for?* It opens us up to receiving by showing us how much we already have.

———— ♦ ————

Pray to your angels in a way that you know what
you're asking for is possible for you.

It's also a really good practice to pray when things are going right, not just when things are going wrong. Make your prayers a priority, not a last resort, or, as I say to my students, "Pray first, not last!"

Pray First, Not Last

All of the ideas we've discussed so far, from raising our vibration to praying first and not last, will bring us into a more positive experience of co-creation with our angels. They are supporting us, but we are actively participating in changing the energy of our spaces. We're helping lift others up. It's important to speak to angels on a daily basis, if you can. Angels are all around you *all the time.*

Angels aren't only found in church. Or hovering over a glorious sunset. They're with you all the time. And, equally important, they're there for you all the time, not only in moments of desperation.

A lot of people only turn to angels when they've tried absolutely everything else. They've exhausted all other avenues to getting what they want. They're approaching angels in a state of depletion, despair, a total lack of abundance. Thinking back to the idea that we want to raise our vibration to interact with angels, how well do you think that will work? Are you really going to turn to your angels only when you're groveling at your lowest point and have nothing to lose? Does that feel like a positive relationship? That's almost worse than the friend who only calls so you can feed his pet.

———————————— ♦ ————————————

Make sure you ask your angels first, not as a
last resort! They're always ready to help.

————————————————————————

When I point this out to people, it's usually pretty clear that's not how they want to be. No one wants to be that person. But sometimes it just takes a bit of a reminder. (That's what I'm here for.)

Our thoughts and emotions are creating our world. How we're approaching the divine is also what we're calling in from the divine. So, if the only way we're talking to angels is as a needy person, that's the experience we're bringing into our life.

I used to do this. I would try everything, and if nothing else worked, when I was at rock bottom, I would start pleading, praying in the style I'd learned in Sunday school: "Dear God, please help me with _____. I hope the future will bring _____."

I think of this style now as a pleading prayer. "Please, Archangel Michael, protect me today." Pleading doesn't always work that well with people, and it doesn't work that well with angels. It isn't that they can't hear you, it's more that pleading is giving off a lower-vibrational energy and there's a fear inside that you cannot be helped.

If you need angelic support, the best way to help this happen is to know that what you are asking for is possible and that you have the capacity to magnetize angelic energy to you by remembering the blessings of your life and what you are grateful for.

A Halo of Light

As you've likely gleaned by now, I love the work of Louise L. Hay, the household name in modern spiritual teaching. Louise's work reminds us that there is no place more powerful than the present moment, and through feeling whole, healed, and complete, we can experience that reality. Louise teaches that our internal beliefs about ourselves are contributors to our lived experience.

Now, I've noticed that a lot of people have been influenced by Louise's work, but have watered down the basics to "Positivity attracts positivity, negativity attracts negativity." I want to point out that this isn't always the case. I also believe that some of this thinking can be damaging, especially for those who have challenges with mental health and anxiety.

I've recently done a video on social media about this, titled: "Your anxiety is not attracting bad experiences," because I have had an influx of messages from followers since the pandemic saying that they are concerned their anxiety is bringing negative energy into their life.

I know deep down that our beliefs and mindset have an impact on our lived experience, but I also believe that if we regularly cultivate a positive vibration through prayer or spiritual practice, that energy will outweigh the moments when we're overwhelmed by negative thoughts. A regular practice of saying, "Thank you, angels," will generate a halo of light that will block the moments of negativity that may sometimes take over your thoughts and mind. It will continue to attract goodness and blessings (just like the prayers of your ancestors).

One of the things I've learned from Louise Hay is there is no place more powerful than the present moment. When we call angels into that moment, we allow ourselves to be supported by them.

Speak "As If"

I love to begin speaking to angels by saying, "Thank you, angels, for reminding me of your presence. It feels so good to know you are here. Thank you for clearing the road ahead." I speak about what I would like as if it had already been done, bringing myself into alignment with a path full of light and wonder. When you approach the conversation with grace, you are bringing yourself closer to love, which is the essence of angels.

> *"Thank you, angels, for reminding me of your*
> *presence. It feels so good to know you are here.*
> *Thank you for clearing the road ahead."*

The moment that convinced me this really worked was my skateboarding accident back in 2012. I'd come tearing down a ramp not made for skateboards and had had quite a fall. It had been caught on film and people had posted it online for days!

My mum told me I needed to go to the hospital.

I am a new thought leader, I thought to myself. *I don't want to be in the hospital.*

Finally, I had no choice but to go.

"Where are you feeling the pain?" the doctors asked.

"I am experiencing the sensation in my knee and my ankle," I told them.

My first book had been published not long before and I'd been on a deep dive in my spiritual practice, trying to find how I could align the ideas of Louise Hay with my prayers to angels.

"He means 'pain,'" my mum translated. "He's trying not to use any negative terminology at the moment."

I had ruptured some ligaments in my knee and ankle and was sent home with a pair of crutches.

That night it dawned on me. I realized I needed to speak as if the healing had already happened.

"Thank you, angels," I said, "for the healing that has already been given to my body. It feels so good to be free and flowing." I must have said it a million times as I lay there that night. "Thank you, angels, for the healing that has already been given to my body."

When you affirm something, your body starts to match it, and there's a good chance you'll become open to receiving it.

As I was saying it, I started to feel the healing. The next morning, I got up, went into the kitchen, started making an omelet, and completely forgot I had the crutches by the side of my bed.

Because I didn't need them.

"I think I've just manifested a miracle," I said.

To myself.

To the angels?

Then I wrote a prayer:

> *"Thank you, angels, for the healing that has already*
> *been given to my knee and ankle. It feels so good*
> *to be free and flowing. All is well in my world."*

I had learned from Louise Hay that knee problems came from not being free and at ease. Those words, "free and flowing," were the ones she used for knee pain.

Speaking "as if" doesn't only work for physical pain. Once someone came to me who was going through a divorce, and instead of asking (or pleading!) for help for them, I said, "Thank you, angels, for placing your hands on this situation and everyone involved. It's so good to have a harmonious resolution." The angels were already there to support and heal, so why not reflect their presence in my words?

Also, people who had tried this way of praying were already reporting miraculous experiences, miraculous encounters.

The woman going through the divorce came back to me later with an update. "Me and my ex weren't talking at all," she said, "then on the day of the divorce he said, 'I don't want any hard feelings.'"

I started trying this approach with everything. When something didn't work out well in one of my professional collaborations, I said: "Thank you, angels, for this relationship. It's now served its purpose. I wish them well on their journey. It feels so good to walk in a separate direction. It feels so good to be doing this on my own and in my own way. Thank you, angels, for supporting this."

For people who couldn't have babies, I said, "Thank you, angels, for supporting me in giving birth to this child. It feels so good to hold my baby in my arms." And they would get pregnant.

More and more, I zoomed in on the *feeling*. One of the things we need to do is let ourselves become aware of our feelings and experience them. I've always been a sensitive person. I feel things big and I know that helps me when it comes to these prayers.

So, how would it feel to have that thing you want actually happen? The rupture healed, the baby born, the divorce settled, the new career opportunity on its way, the loneliness gone?

Take a moment and say, "Thank you, angels, for bearing witness to my prayers and intentions." Just through saying those words I think you will feel the heaviness start to lift.

I started giving this advice out willy-nilly. Anything someone needed help with, I wrote the prayer in that language of feeling and as if it had already happened, as if the Universe was already totally aligned.

And it was.

And then I had to teach people the victory dance, of course! This is something I learned from fellow Hay House author David Hamilton. It's when you dance in a way as if what you are "manifesting" has already happened. Supposedly there's some science out there to show that when you celebrate as if something has already happened, there's an even greater chance of it becoming reality. Plus, celebration is one of the highest spiritual frequencies and supports your prayers being amplified, heard, and answered.

The *feeling* is the miracle. What is the core feeling you're looking to have? Thank the angels and let it happen. When you're fixated on one thing or one way, you're probably limiting yourself to what you think is possible. Your angels may have something else in mind for you. Know that what unfolds will be a pathway to your evolution.

◆ ◆ ◆

So now we can put together some bullet points about how to talk to angels:

- Begin with a thank-you.

- Pray first rather than last.

- Speak as if what you hope for has already happened and imagine what it would feel like. Lean into the feeling.

As you go about your life, remember that angels are with you and thank them for their company. Maybe you'll start noticing more beauty around you; if so, remember to thank the angels for supporting such a lovely world. Maybe you'll notice your neck pain is starting to diminish. Or a grumpy neighbor is waving each morning as he waters his roses.

Angels are always available. Get to know them before you absolutely need them, and you'll have a better chance of good communication when you're in a difficult spot.

Also, if you can remember to thank angels for supporting you when you don't feel you need support, then you'll start to become stronger in your support of other people. The angels would like nothing better.

Grow in love and in awareness. Grow in curiosity. A conversation with angels isn't a script. Start with a feeling. (After the thank-you!)

See where it takes you.

·10·

Angel Signs

"And there in the stillness, in the call to
attention, we just might be saved."

BARBARA MAHANY, THE BOOK OF NATURE:
THE ASTONISHING BEAUTY OF GOD'S FIRST SACRED TEXT[1]

My life is pretty bizarre. If I say the wrong thing, the lights blow. Doors open for no reason. Things bang in another room. High-pitched sounds are everywhere. I hear my name when nobody has called me. Yesterday a big blue light passed through the air in front of me. Angel numbers, like 444, show up all the time in weird and wonderful ways. The other day I was leaving a voice note for my friend Robyn, and the recording was exactly 3:33. Three minutes, 33 seconds—bang on. It's not like I was watching so I could stop it at that time. I was in the car, recording hands-free. It just... happened.

It happens all the time.

I'm constantly reminded there is a presence around me.

When I was at the Spiritualist church, I learned about signs and the many different ways that angels and spirits can send them to us. I found out that angels can use all of our senses and more to direct their loving guidance our way. They'll use what's already around us and draw our attention to it, using our natural sensitivity and intuition.

———————— ♦ ————————

The nature of angels is to communicate and
share reminders of their presence.

I remember when I moved into a really cool loft conversion in Glasgow city center—the first place I could call my own—and a friend came to visit. We had been out for dinner, and we were just relaxing back home in the open-plan living-kitchen area when all the lights started flickering in the kitchen and then the lounge.

"Think we've got a visitor," I said.

"Holy fuck, is someone *actually* there?!"

I asked as well, with perhaps a little more eagerness for the answer to be "yes" than my friend. The lights kept flickering in response.

"Oh, fuck off!" said my friend. "We need to stop this."

I smiled. I am constantly in conversation with the unseen. Angel signs are completely entwined with my life. All the time, I'm being made aware that something bigger is out there. Just today, the code for the gate at the dog park was 3444—a sign that came in as I was writing about signs! It's how I live my life, but still it gives me goosebumps. Angel bumps.

When I was growing up, my grandfather Fred, Mum's dad, used to call himself a silver fox. My mum's brother, Uncle Jim, used to have a CB radio and would use it to speak to people from all around the world. My mum's family would sit round the radio and speak to strangers. Everyone had a codename—my mum's was Lady Godiva and my papa's was Silver Fox.

On my 30th birthday, I got a fox tattooed on my hand. When I moved to the house where I live now, I started seeing a fox every now and then. I called him Freddy Fox and would give him a little food. Now Freddy comes to my door every night with Mrs Fox. When I'm coming home from yoga a little late some evenings (you know, a really wild night out), I see Freddy when I turn off the main road into my community. He'll be out on the main road, but when he sees my car, he runs all the way down and meets me at my house.

When I'm out and about I'm your the-more-the-merrier boy, but I live a very solitary life in many ways. I say my angel prayers. I ride my Peloton bike. I practice kundalini yoga. I care for my mother and look after the dogs. Especially when I'm in book-writing mode, I spend hours alone with my laptop.

Knowing angels are keeping me company gives me a sense of empowerment. Impossible chapter deadline? They're there as I'm banging out the pages. Awkward Zoom meeting? They're cheering me on, helping me remember to breathe through it.

And if I'm ever unsure of their presence, all I have to do is ask for a sign. Angels will send you a sign if you ask for one.

Undeniable Signs

I was doing a reading for a politician once who thought I was pretty talented, but he wasn't so sure about the angel thing. I told him, "You should ask the angels to give you a sign, one that's undeniable."

A day or two later he was giving a speech and reached into his pocket to grab something. Out came a gigantic white feather, wrapped in cellophane. What? A full-size quill feather inside his pocket? In cellophane?

Feathers are angels' calling cards. When you find a feather in an unexplainable place, you have been visited by an angel.

I've got another great story about undeniable signs. About 10 years ago I was going with a group of guys to a music festival in Yorkshire. On the way there, I saw an angel number on the clock, I think it was 11:11, and I said, "Everyone make a wish."

———————— ♦ ————————

The number 11:11 is the ultimate angel message
that you are connected to the Universe and
your prayers will soon be answered.

One of my friends said straight out, "I don't know if I believe in any of that shit."

Another said, "Oh come on, Kyle, you're looking for that sign. That's why you keep finding it." Confirmation bias, he called it.

This was the time I was writing *Angels Whisper in My Ear*. So, I had angels whispering in one ear and my friends doubting it all in the other.

"Fair enough," I said. "Maybe I am. But how about trying an experiment?"

"Sure, why not?"

We decided we would do a little test where I would ask my angels to send us a sign that they were with us.

Well, numbers started coming in like crazy. We stopped at a shop and one of my friends bought drinks (and cigarettes—let's not lie). It came to £5.55. We all went for brunch and split the bill. It was £4.44 each. Everything we did, it was angel numbers everywhere.

"Now this is starting to get really weird," the biggest doubter of all said.

It was undeniable.

Angels will use things around us to get our attention, but I truly believe they have the ability to manifest things as well. In the Spiritualist church when something arrives from nowhere in a séance, it is called an "apport." Was that feather in the politician's pocket put there by angels?

I received an undeniable sign when I was feeling jittery checking into the hotel the first time I was invited to speak abroad, in Hamburg, Germany, 12 years ago. (Actually, rewind: the year before I'd been invited to speak at the Angel Congress in Salzburg, Austria, but the plane ahead of us on the runway had caught fire. They'd closed the runway and we'd never made it out. I ended up doing the speech by Skype.) So, when it came to the Hamburg conference, it was my first international talk truly in person, and I was super-nervous. Who was I to speak in front of all these people? At the time Doreen Virtue was touring as the world's leading angel expert. I was just trying to get established; I wasn't really known. So, I asked for a sign that angels were with me, and when I went to check in, the guy's name was there clearly on his name tag: "Angel."

"Excuse me, can I take a picture of your name tag?"

"Sure."

"Thank you," I said, and then, "Thank you, angels. Thank you for letting me know you're with me and you're part of this journey."

I hope it's clear to you by now that they're part of your journey as well. In every moment of your life, there's a cheerleading squad of love to mirror back to you the love that you are. But I understand that, just like the politician who found the feather, and just like me in Hamburg, you might want an actual sign to know you're on the right path and you're not alone. Have you ever got a sign? How would you know?

How to Recognize a Sign

Sometimes a butterfly is just a butterfly and sometimes it's a divine message. How can you tell when an angel is trying to catch your attention?

———————— ◆ ————————

If your first instinct is "This is a sign," then it is a sign.

Trust your intuition. How do you recognize it? Quite simply, when your intuition is communicating, you'll feel a sense of calm. If you feel anxiety coming over you, or even outright fear, that's not the voice you want to focus your attention on. That kind of negative self-talk will lead you astray. So, give yourself permission to trust your inner voice. This work isn't about handing your power over to someone or something else, but laying claim to the power already inside you.

As you know now, angels are messengers. It's in their nature to get in touch. Unlike some of your friends perhaps, they're not going to leave you on Read. They're like your chatty girlfriend who just won't shut up or an over-eager puppy who greets you like he hasn't seen you in a month when all you did was go to the supermarket. Angels want to keep telling you they are around you. It's not because they want to make you co-dependent in your relationship with them, but rather to assure you you're not alone.

When you see something you think is a sign and you feel connected, you *are*. You don't have to second-guess the feeling, it's a moment that transcends where you are and what you're thinking about. Poet and teacher Mark Nepo has a lovely way to describe it: a moment when "thinking and feeling and knowing and being are all the same."[2]

A lot of us are on the lookout for signs, but so much of the time they show up when we're not looking for them. Our task is to create an openness within that encourages them to manifest. Sure, you can ask the angels to send you a specific sign, but sometimes that means you'll be waiting longer than you'd like. I prefer to hand myself over completely to the angels, and by the grace of God, they'll send something my way that assures me they're close by.

In all honesty, when my journey into this world began, I'd always ask for a sign to know that angels were close by, but as I came to trust them more, I asked less. I discovered very quickly that when you're in constant communication with angels through a daily spiritual practice, you'll be blessed by signs and blown away by how strong they grow to be.

SUMMONING A SIGN

If you would like a sign, here is a little ritual you can try:

Visualize yourself surrounded by golden light. See it moving right over you. This makes your connection to angels even stronger. It's like broadband for your prayers. The basis of this is that we are light in the same way that angels are light. It is through light that we can bring them closer to us and bring ourselves closer to them.

If you find it challenging to visualize, you can say this affirmation instead:

I am immersed in golden light. It has washed over my body from head to toe.

Now say, with loving intentions,

Thank you, angels, for reminding me of your presence!

You can add some gratitude, if you like. This really enhances the angelic connection. I often say:

It feels so good to know you're here. I'm so thankful we're on this journey together!

Now let go and let God! Let the angels bless you with their presence.

Now it's time to move on to what you should *do* when you get a sign.

What to Do About a Sign

Besides listening to the Ace of Base hit "The Sign" on repeat, what should you do when you see a sign? Many people immediately spin themselves into a frenzy trying to figure out what it means. But before we get to interpretation, we should begin with gratitude. You don't want to be that nephew who never mentions the yearly birthday gift and you only know he got it when you see the check has been deposited. So, begin with a thank-you. Here are some simple ways to express it:

- "Thank you, angels, for revealing this sign to me."

- "Thank you, angels, for helping me stay open to your guidance."

- "Thank you, angels, for reminding me that you're there."

- "Thank you, angels, for confirming that I am on the right path."

You may notice that while the first three ideas focus on gratitude for the angels' support, the fourth one differs a bit, suggesting that the sign means you're on the right path. How do you know that to be the case?

It's actually pretty simple to interpret signs, because they all carry one central message, which is exactly that: *You're on the right path. Your intuition is tuned in. Keep going in the direction you're already headed.*

And if you want more specificity, you may be able to get that as well. You can at least ask.

---- ♦ ----

Getting a sign is an opportunity
to pause and ask the angels to reveal
what you need to know.

Even if you don't get anything further than the sign itself, just trust that you're receiving something anyway. Keep growing, keep staying open. Angels want to help you tune in to your own intuition. When you're able to do that, the answers will come.

If you really don't know what to make of a sign, the solution is to let the meaning unfold, to trust that it will.

If you want to, though, why not go directly to the source? The biggest mistake most people make with signs (besides forgetting to say thank you!) is they never ask for the message behind them from the being who sent them their way. Instead, they fret over it alone or ask others, "What do you think this means?" Remember, angels are always there to help us, so thank them for being willing to help you find more meaning in the sign. Then listen for the answer.

Angels love sending signs. They get excited when we recognize them. But it's not like a pop quiz or anything. The signs are meant to show you that angels are with you and to encourage you on your path. If times are tough, receiving a sign means you'll get through it.

All this to say, when you receive a sign, don't squander the moment. It's your cue to slow down and listen. A lot of people will be busy taking a photograph of a cloud shaped like an artichoke, for example, and meanwhile that sacred time is passing them by.

———— ♦ ————

When you receive a sign, you're connecting to angels!

I know I talk about angelic connection like it's an everyday thing—and it is for me and can be for you—but it's also completely amazing. Let's not lose sight of that. There's nothing mundane and ho-hum about talking to angels. Give the conversation your full attention.

Let me recap the points above so when you're in need of a quick refresh you can refer to this list.

First, let signs come to you, don't force them out of hiding. When you do receive a sign:

- Thank the angels.

- Stay present. Don't get distracted uploading a photo to your social media feed. In this moment you are in direct connection with angels.

- Know you are exactly where you need to be.

- Ask for clarification if you like, and whatever further messages you receive, if any, stay aligned and know your path will reveal itself when it is perfect for it to do so.

- If you can, take a few moments to pause and receive any intuitive downloads from the angels.

- You might like to say: "Thank you, angels, for revealing to me what I need to know. I am willing to listen!"

What's Significant?

I should add that while I'm constantly surrounded by signs, I try not to read too much into *everything*. Like the dragonfly that landed in my living room, for example. Dragonfly energy represents going on a journey. When dragonflies keep appearing on our path, angels want us to know that they're with us the whole way. There are loads of blessings surrounding the dragonfly, because it shows we're making huge progress on our journey. But I think that one was just an insect that made its way in from the garden.

A week after the dragonfly came into my living room, a bumblebee came in and landed on my couch. Bumblebees are about gathering in community to heal the world. Could I love that more than I already do? It could be a tagline for one of my online courses. Or all of them.

As bees work together in a community to create honey, they remind us to work together in a team to create positive changes in the world. Also, because bees are so important to the preservation of the Earth, when we see them, angels are thanking us for all the hard work we're doing for others, because it's making the world a better place.

But neither the dragonfly nor the bumblebee felt connected for me. They didn't feel like signs of anything except that maybe I have a hole in the screen and my dogs' nails need a good trim.

I think it's important not to over-interpret potential signs, as that could turn sign-reading into the kind of static noise that makes it harder to hear the true and precious messages from angels. So, let's clear the way for the signs that will resonate and take us further down our spiritual path.

———————————— ♦ ————————————

When it comes to reading signs, stay rooted in
what feels as if it's part of your divine plan.

———————————————————————

I shooed out the dragonfly and the bumblebee without any fanfare, but I will say that nature signs are my favorite. Freddy Fox makes me happy every time I see him, and I always thank the angels for the message from my grandad.

In fact, now is a good time to let you know the meaning behind some of the most common nature signs you might find.

Nature Signs

Angels adore nature, so they can easily work with the laws of nature to send you a message. They can send a shape in a cloud, a vegetable shaped like a love heart, and God only knows what else. I remember my mum found the most perfect heart-shaped potato one night after she'd said some prayers in the kitchen while making dinner. She felt it was a sign that heaven was smiling upon her.

Robins are a lovely nature sign. They bring a message from a loved one in the spirit world, especially during a period of deep grief or if someone has recently passed. The message is: "I am here with you now!"

As robins are territorial little birds, there's a chance they'll visit regularly and make our territory theirs, so they can become the perfect messengers for a departed loved one.

There is one bird that's particularly associated with loved ones sending us a message from beyond, and that's the magpie. These lovely birds have had different meanings over the years. I truly believe they show up to say a loved one is sending their love and watching over us. If we see a cluster of magpies, each one represents a loved one in heaven looking down on us.

Eagles, hawks, and other birds of prey bring a message from the angels to see from a higher perspective. When you see one, you are being encouraged to see the bigger picture, the other person's point of view, and beyond your own personal ideas of what you want, as the Universe is always leading you to your highest, greatest good.

The little red insects called ladybugs or ladybirds are symbols of happiness and peace. Ever since I was a child, I've instinctively known that they're lucky little beings. When they appear in our life, angels want us to know they are present and are smoothing our path.

You'll find interpretations of many more signs, from butterflies to high-pitched noises, below. I should also let you know that you don't have to worry that something is a bad sign.

Many of us have been influenced by superstition and often jump to the worst possible conclusion. I have received hundreds of emails and messages through social media from people who have broken an angel statue while cleaning or have found one being blown over by the wind or similar and worried about its spiritual significance.

I wanted to clear it up, so I asked the angels directly. So I can now say that when you have a broken angel wing, broken angel statue, or similar, angels are taking pain for you or from you. On some level, they are protecting you from a negative experience or drawing pain from you so that you don't have to carry it any longer.

Once when I was having a difficult time, I accidentally knocked over my Archangel Michael statue and his head fell off. I was so upset at first, but upon meditating on it, I heard the clear and insightful message: "The statue lost its head so that you don't have to." The truth was, at that moment of high stress I was "losing my mind." Well, that one was easy to interpret. So, I thanked the angels for sending me a clear sign.

◆

Angels never bring bad omens, only inspiring positive messages that will lead us to the light!

Another neat thing about angel messages is that they can adapt to our changing world. What do I mean by that? Let's jump to that right now.

Angel Adaptation

You know that angels can appear in myriad forms, from a hazy orb of light to a blue triangle to a woman walking down a country road in the dark. Not only are they adept at changing form, but they are also constantly updating their language so they can reach us through all the new ways we use to communicate.

When we start aligning ourselves with the frequency of angels and noticing signs around us, we'll likely notice that many of them are quite modern. Repeated numbers on our smartphone. A streaming show suggested for us that relates exactly to the guidance we need. Notifications from an app. The printer acting strange. Smart lights flickering. A typo that reveals something we need to know. A mistake on GPS taking us the wrong way that turns out to be the right way. Angels love to use what we have around us and a lot of the time that's electronics, so when things don't work properly, don't be surprised. You're receiving a visit!

I've experienced my phone turning itself on and off, channels changing, and other weird occurrences where my laptop sticks on an angel picture with an important message. At the moment I keep getting TikTok notifications from a young woman who took her own life not long ago. "Click here to be her friend," they keep telling me. Clearly, she is trying to get in touch with me, right? But I'm not even on TikTok. For now, I'm stumped as to what to make of it. Still, I know that what I need to know and what I need to do will be revealed in a perfect time–space sequence. What I need to do in the meantime is to make sure my actions, choices, and life are aligned to the frequency of this higher love.

I know it may seem strange to think of angels communicating through this high-tech world of ours, but remember they're timeless. This age of the smartphone is just a blip on their timescale. To them, the Stone Age, which lasted several million years, was just a blip as well. A long blip, maybe. But a blip.

So, angels are sending us messages using everything around us, but here's the big question—are we listening?

Are You Listening?

Sometimes angels do speak loud and clear. One woman I met was driving down the highway when a voice from nowhere said, "Move into the next lane." Without hesitation, she switched lanes, just as debris began to fall from the back of the truck that had been ahead of her in the previous lane. Her life was saved by deciding to listen to that voice. She'd had the choice to ignore it, but because she listened, her life was saved. This gave her a new reason to live, a new reason to be grateful, and the feeling that she was connected to something greater. The experience confirmed to her she could live in a more purposeful way.

Have you ever got a message like that?

I've met countless people in my life who have heard a voice warning them: "Don't do it," "Don't go there," "Wait an extra hour before you leave," "Don't trust that person." But some people ignore voices for years. How many people are in a relationship they maybe should have ended 10 years ago? How many people are on their way to a job they wanted to leave the moment they started it? So many of us aren't listening. We've been taught to ignore our feelings and our intuition and not upset people. So, we learn to tune those voices out.

This goes back to what I said before about intuition and trusting our hunches.

When we want to hear angels, we first of
all have to listen to ourselves.

Although many times we don't listen to the voice inside us, I've found that often in a life-or-death moment, there's a quietness that comes over us. In those windows of dramatic change, the inner voice can be louder than ever. If something is going to be really bad for us, I think we'll get that, and we'll know it's not our time to go.

I wrote for the magazine *Women's World* for four or five years, reviewing angel stories. While writing that column, I noticed that in a lot of the stories people had a choice when the question of life or death presented itself; they could decide whether they took their angel's hand or not. How many people heard that voice but didn't listen and aren't here now?

First, angels will try to reach us on the inside, sending a message through our own heart. But if we're not listening, they have to try other ways of getting our attention. (They don't give up easily.) So, they will leave a feather or a coin, or send a magpie or a ladybug. The signs will get more obvious from there. Eventually they'll use a megaphone or its equivalent—like a car cutting in front of us with the message we need on its bumper sticker or the UPS driver showing up with his name tag saying Raphael.

Still, some people don't want the responsibility implied by hearing from an angel. My friend Stephen, for example, doesn't believe in anything. Although even he tells me, "There's something spooky about you. Definitely something a bit weird." Can't argue with that. If you ask me, I'd say he's not really willing to think deeply about just what that spookiness is or where it comes from. That would require responsibility and perhaps a step down a spiritual path. And that path isn't always an easy one.

This is a theme I'm trying to bring forward through this book. Even though I want to show you how much light and love angels can bring to your life, it's not all light and love, because we are humans here on Earth. Angels aren't here to take away our human experience.

The truth is that many of us are struggling. And the most devoted and mystical people struggle too. That was a big wake-up call for me when I started to be part of the spiritual speaking circuit—those famous mediums, psychics, and channelers I looked up to on TV and in books and magazines all had normal day-to-day challenges like everyone else. But for me, the more human people become, the more holy they seem to be.

People are dealing with all kinds of issues all the time. Fortunately, over the past several years we've been gaining more awareness about some of the things people are facing in their lives.

This is what I think of when I say we can hold out for a miraculous happening. Which leads me to another sign.

Rainbows

I don't know if you remember that earlier I mentioned my mum's sister, my aunt June, who looked after me a lot when my mum was working. She was the one who married a pastor, and it was his church that I first attended when I was growing up. By that point June was a devout Christian, but she'd been a bit psychic when she was younger and read the tea leaves for family and friends.

At the Sunday school I attended at that church, they told us the story of Noah. At the end, there's a rainbow after the Flood, a promise from God that things will get better from here on out. That message was embedded into my heart from an early age. And here I am still, always holding out for a miracle.

June believed that when she saw a rainbow, God was answering her prayers. Her faith added to what I had learned from watching my neighbor Margaret's prayers in her church. From June, I understood that when you said a prayer, some kind of answer was going to come, it just might not be in spoken form. It might be a sign.

Aunt June passed away three years ago and to this day when I see a rainbow, I think of her.

When we see rainbows all around us, it's a promise from the Universe that our prayers will soon be answered. Rainbows encourage us to have faith, because angels have faith in us. Rainbows are a sign that our prayers have been heard.

Other Signs from Angels

As we've learned, angels love to let the world know they are close by and will do anything within their power to send a "wink" from heaven. Over the years I've made a note of the signs that they send our way so that we can know they are close to us. Here are some more of them, together with their meanings.

Angel statues, figures, confetti, or similar

Finding an angel statue, figure, confetti, or similar means angels are closer than we think. When we come across an angel-shaped item, for example a piece of angel confetti on our shoe or on a table in a restaurant, or an angel figurine in the park, it's our angels telling us that they are with us, can hear our prayers, and are doing everything within their power to help us on our journey.

Angelic symbols

Angels love little symbols and they love using them to tell us they're present. They can make us notice things in our daily life that look like wings, feathers, or even the outline of an angel.

Butterflies

Butterflies are a favorite angel sign and have a dual meaning. The butterfly has long been known as a symbol of transformation, and I've found that butterflies arrive on our path when we're going through great change and overcoming previous challenges. However, I've also found they come to us when we've lost a loved one who went through pain. That loved one is letting us know they've overcome the diseases of the Earth and are now free.

Coins

I've always believed that coins represent loved ones in heaven, in particular grandparents. It's as though they're coming through and offering us a little shiny penny to give us a push in the right direction and wish us luck.

Dolphins

Dolphins are some of the angels' most treasured beings on Earth. They are the angels of the sea. Dolphins represent family, freedom, and deep bonds of friendship and trust. When we see them, angels are with us, encouraging us to have fun, be free, and enjoy the friends and family we have around us.

Feathers

Feathers are the best-known angel signs. Angels absolutely love sending them to us. Finding a feather is like being given an angelic business card or love note. The feathers can be any color, but sometimes the color has a message of its own:

- *Black:* Your angels are absorbing your pain or any other challenging emotions you are currently dealing with. Take some time to ask for the extra support you need and deserve from heaven.

- *Blue:* Your angels are encouraging you to open up and be honest.

- *Green:* Your angels want to acknowledge your capacity to give, share, and love without conditions.

- *Indigo/Purple:* Your current experiences are providing a spiritual awakening.

- *Orange:* Your angels are placing a light of harmony and wellness around you. Self-care is essential at this time.

- *Pink:* You are surrounded by unconditional love at this time.

- *Red:* Your angels are supporting you on a physical level to help you get together everything you need in order to feel safe and supported.

- *White:* Your guardian angel wants you to know they're close by and they know about your prayers and/or current situation. They're asking you to remain positive.

- *Yellow:* Your angels are encouraging you to focus on what is good, light, and supportive for you at this time.

Hearing our name

Hearing our name being called when no one is there is a call to action. It's the angels giving us a reminder that the answer we are seeking is in fact within and never to underestimate the power we have within us.

This experience can often happen when we're drifting off to sleep or just waking up in the morning, because the state between sleep and waking consciousness is a window that allows us to open up to other planes of existence.

Ultimately, hearing our name being called is the Universe/God echoing the love that it has for us and reminding us of the love that is within us.

───────── ♦ ─────────

The power, influence, and positivity we have
within can help heal and change the world.

─────────────────

High-pitched noises

Hearing a high-pitched noise is what I now call a "download." I believe these buzzing sounds in our ears (given that we don't have tinnitus) mean we are picking up on a frequency beyond our body and even beyond this realm. I like to imagine that we are like huge walking radios or computers that are constantly receiving signals from heaven. I feel that when I hear a high-pitched noise, I am downloading information, and often it'll be the answer to a prayer.

These downloads need to be unzipped, just like a computer file, and via meditation we can invite our angels to unlock the information for us so that we can follow the guidance.

Money

When we continually find money in random places, on our path, or even in clothing we've not worn in a while, angels are sending us financial support and security. We're being asked to open up all channels to receive the abundance we truly deserve.

Music

Angels love music. In fact, they're the most incredible singers. There's a category of angels called the Seraphim who are said to sing the praises of the Creator constantly. I've woken up many times to the most beautiful sounds and songs that have no other explanation than an angelic one. Angels love music so much, they allow it to be their messenger.

Our angels will often encourage us to turn on the radio, change the channel, or walk into a shop when a specific song is playing, so we can get a message from the lyrics or the title.

Remember how I heard the Destiny's Child song "Survivor" as I was doing the reading at the barbecue? When the angels gave me that song that summer evening, they were coming up with something they knew would catch my attention and help translate the message they were trying to give.

When we hear a song over and over again, we're being asked to pay careful attention—there's a message for us there.

———————————— ♦ ————————————

Ask your angels to speak to you through music
the next time you need an answer.

———————————————————————

I have a friend who often hears a song connected to a lost loved one at the very moment she needs to hear from them or know that they're with her. She doesn't call it an angel message, but it's pretty miraculous timing!

Stars

Seeing stars everywhere we go is a message from heaven thanking us for a job well done. Angels want us to know that they're aware of our achievements and the transformations we've made, and they're so proud of us.

Winged creatures

Angels have been seen and depicted as winged creatures and they work closely with the animal and insect realm to send us messages through other winged creatures. Everything from bees to birds can bring us messages from the angels and the spirit world.

Words

Angels love using words too. Have you ever noticed a word you just needed to hear while driving along the road? Have you ever seen a van pulling in front of you with the message you needed right at that moment? Well, angels have sent those messages.

· 11 ·

Can Humans Become Angels?

"All God's angels come to us disguised."

JAMES RUSSELL LOWELL

Now we come to one of the most popular questions when it comes to understanding angels: Can humans become angels?

As I've written earlier, I came into the world of angels after many of the rules had been set. For most angel experts, humans were humans, angels were angels, and that was that.

I questioned that distinction. (Noticing any common themes here?) I genuinely felt that when loved ones died, they lived on, but I wasn't sure in what form. Could my grandmother have become an angel?

Now, when it comes to our *guardian* angels, I've always believed we have one for our whole lifetime and starting well before our lifetime on Earth begins. So, it wouldn't make sense, for example, for my grandmother to pop off and become my guardian angel when she passed away, because I already had one. But as to whether humans can become angels, I'm not convinced the lines are as clear-cut as other angel experts believe.

Scripture can guide us here. In the Book of Tobit (or Tobias in some versions) there's a group of exiled Jews, including a man named Tobit. (This is around the second century BCE, so these would be diaspora Jews whose ancestors had been exiled from Israel by the Assyrians some five centuries earlier.) He is in a group traveling along a road when a man falls sick and is blinded by this sickness. A man who is actually Archangel Raphael but looks like a normal guy says essentially, "Behold, I am an angel of the Lord. I will heal this man." So, this tells us that angels can disguise themselves as humans.

In Scripture, angels disguise themselves as humans.
Have you entertained angels unawares?

What about the souls of humans becoming angels? This is the question that interests many people who are hoping to connect with family members they have lost. The Kabbalistic texts suggest that Archangel Metatron was once the prophet Enoch, who was the great-grandfather of Noah. I've always been fascinated by Enoch. A lot of mystery surrounds this figure, and you know how much I like mystery. We don't learn that much about him, and the Book of Enoch was left out of the canon and considered part of the Apocrypha. (Protestants also left out the Book of Tobit. Other traditions include it.)

So, let me tell you Enoch's story.

Born in the Fertile Crescent in the time before the Flood, Enoch kept his attention on God throughout his life and on things unseen and eternal. And one day he just... joined God. In Genesis we learn "Enoch walked faithfully with God; then he was no more, because God took him away."[1] Enoch didn't die, he was simply taken away. It is said he became an angel, maybe even an archangel.

Enoch's ascent brings to mind the story of Mother Mary. It is said that she didn't die either, she was simply lifted up by angels and "assumed" into heaven. In today's world, she's regarded as the queen of the angels, and for me she is an angel.

So, we've got Raphael disguising himself as a human to help a sick man, and we've got a couple of Jews being lifted straight up to heaven by angels at the end of their lives. Did they become angels?

In *A Course in Miracles*, angels and humans are both described as the "thoughts of God." Based on this epithet, it might be fair to conclude that there is no difference between angels and humans, except humans have an ego and angels are pure beings of love, beyond all fear and hate.

So, where does this get us in terms of the question guiding this chapter? Does it mean humans can become angels?

Um, maybe?

I say that a little bit jokingly, and yet I know it needs an answer. Especially when the person asking me is a parent who has lost a child. Who am I to tell them that child isn't watching over them the way an angel would? Who am I to say any loved one isn't going to go on and become an angel? Who am I to take that solace away?

♦ ♦ ♦

One reading I did transformed my thinking about this issue. Up until that point I was okay going along with what everyone else was saying. I was just winging it—pun intended.

And then I met Nessa.

I started the reading and got a message right away. "Do you have two daughters?" I asked.

"No, I've only got one," said Nessa.

I was hearing the message: "She has a daughter in heaven."

"Did you lose a child?" I asked gently.

"Yes, I lost a little girl."

I stayed open to the messages I was receiving. "I've got an angel here," I said to Nessa, "and it's telling me it's your daughter. She keeps telling me she's your angel."

And then I felt the words "my angel."

Nessa showed me a picture of the headstone of her daughter, who had been stillborn. On it were the words: "My angel."

That's where my practice of calling in "my angel" came from. I first shared this practice publicly at an event in London and I was wowed by the response. I remember looking up and seeing so many people in deep spaces, and many with tears of joy running down their faces because all the pretentious stuff had dropped away.

So many of us put ourselves under psychic pressure to experience angels either through visions or hearing their voice, when really the most important skill to develop is the ability to feel their loving presence.

Just saying those magic words internally or out loud (whatever feels good for you) opens your heart and allows your loving angel to draw closer than ever. Try it now:

> Activate your energy by rubbing your palms together vigorously (or whatever feels good for you).
>
> Then, with warm hands, place one hand on your heart and one hand on your belly.
>
> Take several deep breaths.

When you feel you've slowed down, say the invocation below. After each line, close your eyes and allow yourself to feel all the feelings that come up for you.

I call upon my angel.

I welcome in the presence of my angel.

My angel I welcome here.

It feels so good to be connected to my angel.

My angel is with me now.

My angel is guiding me on my way.

I am protected by my angel.

I am protected by my angel.

I am protected by my angel.

And so it is.

Use this practice as often as you like—let your angel come close and hold you through the good days and the challenging days. Your angel is with you. You are their purpose. They are there for you.

That reading brought me that beautiful practice. Meeting Nessa and meeting her daughter, in angel form, also showed me that departed loved ones, especially children, can become angelic figures that watch over their family.

In some Japanese Buddhist traditions, loved ones can become personal Buddhas after death.[2] We see something similar in many different belief systems all over the world. The *Día de los Muertos* (Day of the Dead) in Mexico is a traditional holiday in the autumn that celebrates the continued connection between those who have passed on to another world and those who are still here. Beautiful altars called *Ofrendas* are created with candles, flowers, and items that have particular meaning for the loved ones now in the spirit world who will hopefully pay the living a visit. The reunion is joyful.

Many traditions around the world hold the spirits of their departed loved ones close in various ways. I'm honored I can sometimes serve as a go-between. For Nessa, who lost her daughter at birth, I hope our reading provided her some small comfort. I know it will never make up for what she lost.

I have seen so much loss in my years of doing private one-to-one readings. What do people come to me hoping to find? So often, of course, it's loved ones they've lost. And it's brutal. I know it feels all spooky and wild to get in touch with beings from the other side. Sometimes it's treated like carnival entertainment: "Step right up and meet your angel!" But so much pain and loss is revealed in doing spiritual work—and being alive. That's one of the reasons I'm so keen to avoid toxic positivity. It just doesn't help. And it's hardly a grounded perspective. Not while we have groups whose land has been taken from them, people who have been oppressed for centuries and still are, people who are being horribly mistreated, sidelined, scared. People dealing with all kinds of illnesses, including those that are invisible to others. People working to overcome disability. People living in war zones or facing famine or natural disasters.

And then there was that woman standing in front of me, showing me the picture of her daughter's grave. The daughter she never got to see grow up.

———————————— ♦ ————————————

I believe the souls of lost children become
angels for their parents.

————————————————————————————————

I believe any loved one might go on to become a guide in some way. And we can find all kinds of comfort in knowing our loved ones who have passed to the other side are still somehow by *our* side. Who am I to take that away from anyone? I may spend a lot of my time hanging out with angels, but I'm not one of them. I know what it's like to lose. All of this was born out of the loss of my nana and the breaking apart of my family when I'd only been on this planet a few short years.

♦ ♦ ♦

I want to tell the story of another loved one who paid me a remarkable visit. I call this "the Coney Island story," although when I first heard the words "Coney Island" (during this reading), I had no idea where or what it was. I wondered if it was a remote island in the middle of the ocean. I was pleasantly surprised to learn that it's like the Brighton Pier of New York. Rides, candy floss, and seaside snacks. How pleasant!

Okay, so I was in the Glasgow meeting room that I was renting at the time. It was in a building in the city center where you could rent a private office on a day rate. In my hometown, people came for readings at my house, but I would meet other people in the city and charge a higher rate.

It was the end of November or early December, and the Christmas lights were coming on in the city center that night. The festive streets were full of people, and a woman called Wendy came into my windowless office.

As I was tuning in to do the reading, I saw two angels in my mind, like two golden lights. I felt that they were bringing this woman's mother through to us.

Wendy was excited when she heard that.

The woman who came had sandy-colored hair in a kind of long bowl cut. I described her to Wendy and she nodded. "Yes, that's my mother."

I told her, "Well your mother feels well and she's happy." But then I heard a sound that was a little troubling, and I asked, "Did she have emphysema?"

"Yes, that's right," said Wendy.

"Well, she wants you to know she's no longer in pain and she wants to talk to you about your two sisters."

"I've only got one sister."

I relayed that to the angels, but they kept saying, "Two sisters. Two sisters."

"I'm being told to say to you you've got two sisters. Why is that so strong? Is it two daughters? What's the two?"

"I don't know. I only have one sister."

I decided just to let it go. When I get things wrong, that's usually what I do—I let it go and sometimes ask the client to make a note of it. That's what I was planning to do then when Wendy cut in.

"It's really weird that you say that."

"Okay," I said. "Why?"

"My sister lives in Canada and she recently went to see a shamanic practitioner."

At that time I didn't really know anything about shamanism. I have since discovered that shamans are found in most cultures and traditions, and are basically spirit workers, healers, and psychics who work with the Earth and spirit beings to help others.

"He told her we have a sister out there."

"That *is* odd," I said. "I'll try to get more information for you."

I wrote down what came to me:

> *"May Brown.*
> *Coney Island, New York.*
> *Miriam."*

I handed the piece of paper to Wendy. "This might tell you more about it if you want to do more research."

"Thank you."

We continued the reading and went on to other subjects. I finished my scheduled readings and enjoyed the Christmas lights on George Square before heading home.

I forgot about the reading until a few weeks later when my editor at the *Scottish Sun* said, "Did you tell a woman that she had a sister?"

I shrugged. Someone had a sister? Sounded like a pretty common event. "I don't know," I said.

"Did you do a reading where you told someone she had a sister she didn't *know* about?"

"That seems familiar," I said.

"They fucking found her! They found her sister!" The editor was really wound up about it.

Wendy had written in to the paper to tell us the story and given her phone number, and I rang her up straightaway.

"I tried to get in touch with you," she told me, "but you're impossible to get hold of, so I thought, *I'll just write to the* Sun."

"Okay," I said. "What's the story?"

It turned out that before Wendy was born, her mother had another child. She was only young at the time and the woman who delivered the baby, whose name was May Brown, told her she had died on arrival, but the newborn was actually sold on the black market before ending up with a Jewish family on Coney Island, New York. The adoptive family didn't know the mother had been told a lie. Apparently I'd written her sister's name down exactly. Sarah had grown up not resembling the rest of the family and wondered why. One day she went to see a psychic and was told, "Your birth mother is in heaven and your two sisters are looking for you."

So, all three sisters had gone to psychics of one sort or another and the mother had come through to them all in different ways but with the same information. The souls of departed loved ones reside in the same place as angels and can work with them to bring harmony and healing to those on the Earth, and this was a great example of it.

Both of those stories centered around a lost baby, one who was lost to this world before birth, and one who was lost to her mother and sisters and later found. I'd love to say this is the happy ending story. In some ways it is. The sisters were reunited thanks to the mother's persistence after death. But they clashed in personality, and last I heard they hadn't been able to work it out. I wish I could leave that part of the story out and end on a high note, but you know, *authenticity*. And our human world is a messy one, isn't it?

♦ ♦ ♦

Before I lose the thread of my argument, let me review where we are. From the Apocryphal texts to the woman whose daughter was an angel to the three sisters whose mother came through with angels, there's quite a bit to suggest that the lines between humans and angels aren't quite as clear-cut as many angel experts would have you believe.

For as many answers as we come upon, there will always be new questions. Based on what I've learned and experienced in my life, I now think maybe humans can be angels. But I'd like to end this chapter by telling you something I do know for sure: angels have been with us for our whole lifetime. From the moment we were born, and even before that. Your guardian angel is a being of light that has been with you since before you incarnated.

Before we had our families, we had our angels. That's how old our angels are. Before we had this life, and these bodies, I believe we danced among the stars with angels. The call to connect with our angel in this life might be seen as spiritual interest, a desire to heal, a longing to go deeper. But I believe it is also the unearthing of a memory of what was here before this body.

───────────── ♦ ─────────────

By connecting with our angel, we're tapping
into a memory of a time before we were
born, something sacred and ancient.

Sometimes we can't put our finger on why we feel called to learn about these beings and why we know they're out there. There's not a lot of evidence, nothing scientific to prove the existence of angels, no matter how much we long for it. But something makes us feel that they are real, and I believe that feeling is the result of having connected with them already. That's why, although they might feel intimidating at first when they visit us, they are also familiar. That's why we feel an immediate kind of harmony with them, like a song we remember from early childhood, before our grandmother died, before our father left. The tune is held deep in our bones, even if we can't string together the words.

We are not so very far from angels; they've always been beside us. They are something we are remembering from when we were in heaven. When we welcome angels, we're welcoming them *back*. Returning to who we were. Going home. To a place of protection.

You Always Have a Choice

Some fields, like maths, have clear answers. To begin with, at least. When you get further along in mathematics, you get to a more nebulous realm. As you might remember, I didn't get that far. I walked out of maths class and out of formal schooling altogether when I was 16. Speaking of which, I don't think I told you the rest of the story.

I was the first to arrive home that day. Mum was working a back shift at the airport until 10 p.m., so I gave her a call.

"I've walked out of school," I blurted out as soon as she picked up the phone.

"Did you get out early?"

"No," I said. "I'm not going back."

Mum told me I had one week to find a job. I think she was hoping to scare me into going back to school. But instead, I read the job postings in the local newspaper and saw that a hair salon was opening up a holistic spa and looking for assistants to join their new space. I decided I would walk in and see if I could get a position. I started the following Monday.

After I had washed people's hair, I would give them a massage. I always kept my angel cards in my apron pocket and would let the clients pick one for inspiration and then give them a mini-reading if they were open to it. The owners loved it because I kept their clients entertained. I made £60 a week for 39 hours, plus tips, which I got because of my epic massage and card-reading skills.

Certain things can take me right back to that time. Like the smell of the angel cards—my first deck, now held together by scotch tape. The smell takes me back even further actually, to my 15th birthday and to the bookshop with tarot cards and many lovely magical things. It was the Borders in the center of Glasgow's Buchanan Street. How I adored that giant four-floored shop where people would take shelter from the rain, meet friends, have a coffee in the café, and, of course, buy books.

I'd been a bit lost before I picked that first card, *Synchronicity*. Although who isn't a bit lost coming up to 15? It's a time of intense metamorphosis. It certainly was for me.

Another time of rapid change was when I'd been DJing and working at the hotel and then saw the white feather fall out of the Diana Cooper book on angels. Then I saw my own guardian angel, and finally I got the call from the *Scottish Sun* asking me to be an angel columnist. That was when I turned back to the angel path.

A couple weeks after I started the newspaper job, I went to meet the editor-in-chief, or as everyone called him, "the big boss." Although this was the guy on top, he was a lot pleasanter and more approachable than the features editor to whom I'd been reporting.

"Welcome to the *Scottish Sun*, Kyle!" he said, taking me into his office, which was on the top floor, with frosted glass doors and an incredible view of Glasgow's rooftops.

"I thought it would be worthwhile having a chat before we introduced you to our readers. As you know, the *News of the World* Group are well known and we can't risk any of our columnists having secrets they don't want the world to know about."

Oh, God, I thought to myself. Everyone's going to find out I'm...

"So, let's hear it," he said. "Any skeletons in the closet?"

Well, not really any skeletons, just the fact that I *myself* was in the closet. I decided I would go home and come out to my mum immediately. I didn't want her to hear it from anyone but me. No one would expose me—I would open up myself.

At home Mum was sprawled across the beige leather sofa, watching her usual housewives' shows.

"I've got something to chat to you about." I sat down beside her.

Mum turned off the TV and sat up on the couch so she was facing me.

"I'm gay, Mum," I said. "And I wanted to tell you first."

"I know you are," she said. "I've had an idea for a while, ever since you told me you were unsure when you were younger."

I didn't say anything, but tears of relief started to roll down my cheeks.

"Thank you for telling me," Mum said. "Nothing will ever change how much I love you."

The truth is, no one was all that interested in my sexuality, neither the big boss nor the *Sun* readers. But I didn't know that. I had only just begun to come to terms with it myself. I didn't even really start dating until a few years later, when I was 24. Remember that hypothetical person I wrote about a while back who was gay and everyone knew it but them? And then they really started to shine once they embraced who they were? Maybe that person was me.

What I felt then is what I know now: *I want to do a good job for the angels*. If I'm not authentic, I'm not going to be able to do that work. I *have* to be authentic, even if that makes me vulnerable. Otherwise, there's going to be a block. There will be static in the channel. How can I write about the importance of authenticity and not embrace who I am?

♦ ♦ ♦

Remember I told you that I'd been picking the same card over and over recently? That card is the angel Amethyst: *Metamorphosis*. I pull it, put it back, shuffle, pull it again. Same thing the next day. If you're getting a sign over and over, that sign is to highlight something you need to heal, to change, to embrace, or to let go of... So I know once again I'm in a transformative time in my work and my life.

That doesn't necessarily mean that I have to go bigger. Already I've turned down some exciting opportunities. I worry that I could be stepping onto a pedestal and maybe giving the impression I can see what others can't see. That isn't true, as you know now. And what's more, *seeing* angels isn't as important as *experiencing* them, however that happens.

Even though I've been considered an "expert" on angels for a while now, every day I'm uncovering information that is leading me to a deeper and even more profound experience of these mysterious beings. I've tried my best to describe some of my encounters in this book, but no description I can offer you will ever really do justice to what it's like to be aware of the presence of an angel.

I once had the choice to walk out of a maths classroom or stay where I was. The choice to embrace angels or set them aside. Mary of Nazareth had a choice. The woman on the highway who was told to change lanes had a choice. Ezekiel had a choice, and he chose to pass along the vision he had received.

Connecting with angels offers a path toward healing, devotion, and love. It's the most powerful path I know. But you always have a choice. Earlier I wrote about how people stand to gain by keeping us unaware of our power. Welcoming an angel into your experience isn't a loss of power, whatever you might have been told. It will give you *more* control over your life, more choices, more clarity, and more love.

I no longer live in a gritty seaside town on Inverclyde. In my twenties I moved to the city, and since that time my mum and dad have both left as well. Now I find myself in a quiet town tucked between the city and the mountains. You can see Glasgow if you get high enough up the hill, but mostly you see trees and lochs.

The weather is often wild. But inside there is a calm space and the truth I've always known: we aren't the only ones here. Sharing angels with others brings me into deeper communion with them myself. I don't know what's on the other side of this current metamorphosis, but I do know that I'm grateful for the invitation to be a part of the light and love and healing in the world.

Will you join me?

Remember, you always have a choice.

And whatever you choose, angels are with you.

Angels are with you now.

References

Chapter 2: Do Not Be Afraid

1. Warner, M. (2013), *Alone of All Her Sex: The Myth and Cult of the Virgin Mary*. Oxford: Oxford University Press.

2. Andrew, E. J. (2005), *Writing the Sacred Journey: The Art and Practice of Spiritual Memoir*. Boston: Skinner House Books.

Chapter 3: Who Are Angels?

1. AP-Norc at the University of Chicago (2023), 'The University of Chicago: The May 2023 AP-NORC Center Poll': https://apnorc.org/wp-content/uploads/2023/07/May-Omnibus-2023-Topline-Belief-in-Angels-.pdf [Accessed September 20, 2024]

2. McKeithen, L. (2023), 'New survey finds over half of Americans believe angels exist': www.beliefnet.com/columnists/christnewstoday/2023/08/new-survey-finds-over-half-of-americans-believe-angels-exist.html [Accessed September 20, 2024]

3. Guerin, S. and Bigley, N. (2023), 'Angelic Encounters Study Results': https://static1.squarespace.com/static/6431b0f54521691153def4f0/t/659b68b2f6b7f77b0b131ca4/1704683698918/Angelic+Encounters+Study+Results+2023.pdf [Accessed September 9, 2024]

4. The Bible Society (2016), 'A third of all Brits believe in guardian angels': www.biblesociety.org.uk/latest/news/a-third-of-all-brits-believe-in-guardian-angels [Accessed September 9, 2024]

5. Moorjani, A. (2012), *Dying to Be Me: My Journey from Cancer, to Near Death, to True Healing*, Carlsbad, CA: Hay House.

6. *Ibid.*, p.154.

Chapter 5: Angels through the Ages

1. Ezekiel 1:1–4, Holy Bible, New International Version: https://tinyurl.com/5xzwypym [Accessed June 20, 2024]

2. Reburn, L. and Tresniowski, A. (2023), *The Girl Who Saw Heaven: A Fateful Tornado and a Journey of Faith.* New York: Simon & Schuster, p.87.

3. *Ibid.,* p.88.

Chapter 8: Attracting Angels

1. Kosloski, P. (2017), 'Who composed the "Angel of God" prayer?': https://aleteia.org/2017/10/02/who-composed-the-angel-of-god-prayer [Accessed September 20, 2024]

2. Donnelly, D. (2007), 'Lovingly Observant: An interview with Susannah Heschel': www.americamagazine.org/issue/618/article/lovingly-observant [Accessed April 1, 2024]

Chapter 9: Speaking to Angels

1. Williamson, M. (1996), *A Return to Love: Reflections on the principles of* A Course in Miracles. San Francisco: HarperOne.

Chapter 10: Angel Signs

1. Mahany, B. (2023), *The Book of Nature: The Astonishing Beauty of God's First Sacred Text.* Minneapolis, MN: Broadleaf Books.

2. Nepo, M. (2024), *The Little Book of Awakening: 52 Weekly Selections.* Newburyport, MA: Red Wheel, p.54.

Chapter 11: Can Humans Become Angels?

1. Genesis 5:25, Holy Bible, New International Version: https://tinyurl.com/3h7y6wdd [Accessed September 20, 2024]

2. Arai, P. and Iyer, P. (2023), *The Little Book of Zen Healing: Japanese Rituals for Beauty, Harmony, and Love.* Boulder, Colorado: Shambala.

Bob Rafferty

About the Author

Kyle Gray has had spiritual encounters from an early age. When he was just four years old, his grandmother's soul visited him from the other side. Growing up, Kyle always had an ability to hear, feel, and see what goes beyond the natural senses, which eventually led him to discover the power of angels and spiritual energy in his teens.

Now Kyle is one of the world's leading angel experts who dedicates his life to helping others discover their spiritual abilities. With his sharp wit, need for truth, and remarkable intuitive gifts, he has become one of the most sought-after teachers within his field and speaks to sell-out crowds across the globe. Kyle believes that spiritual connection is possible for everyone, and he's dedicated to helping people shift their energy and deepen their relationship with the divine.

Kyle is based in Glasgow, Scotland, and he's a senior yoga teacher with Yoga Alliance Professionals. Kyle teaches through online training courses and Angel Team Community and is the best-selling author of nine books and the cocreator of nine oracle card decks.

kylegray.co.uk

@kylegrayuk

@kylegrayuk

@kylegrayuk

We hope you enjoyed this Hay House book. If you'd like to receive our online catalog featuring additional information on Hay House books and products, or if you'd like to find out more about the Hay Foundation, please contact:

Hay House LLC, P.O. Box 5100, Carlsbad, CA 92018-5100
(760) 431-7695 or (800) 654-5126
www.hayhouse.com® • www.hayfoundation.org

———

Published in Australia by:
Hay House Australia Publishing Pty Ltd
18/36 Ralph St., Alexandria NSW 2015
Phone: +61 (02) 9669 4299
www.hayhouse.com.au

Published in the United Kingdom by:
Hay House UK Ltd
1st Floor, Crawford Corner,
91–93 Baker Street, London W1U 6QQ
Phone: +44 (0)20 3927 7290
www.hayhouse.co.uk

Published in India by:
Hay House Publishers (India) Pvt Ltd
Muskaan Complex, Plot No. 3,
B-2, Vasant Kunj, New Delhi 110 070
Phone: +91 11 41761620
www.hayhouse.co.in

———

Let Your Soul Grow

Experience life-changing transformation—one video
at a time—with guidance from the world's leading experts.

www.healyourlifeplus.com

MEDITATE.
VISUALIZE.
LEARN.

With the **Empower You**
Unlimited Audio *Mobile App*

Unlimited access to the entire Hay House audio library!

You'll get:

- 600+ inspiring and life-changing **audiobooks**

- 1,000+ ad-free **guided meditations** for sleep, healing, relaxation, spiritual connection, and more

- Hundreds of audios **under 20 minutes** to easily fit into your day

- **Exclusive content** *only* for subscribers

- **New audios** added every week

- No credits, **no limits**

Listen to the audio version of this book for **FREE!**

★★★★★ **Life changing.**
❝ My fav app on my entire phone, hands down! – Gigi ❞

Scan me with your phone camera!

TRY FOR FREE!
Go to: hayhouse.com/listen-free

HAY HOUSE
Online Video Courses

Your journey to a better life starts with figuring out which path is best for you. Hay House Online Courses provide guidance in mental and physical health, personal finance, telling your unique story, and so much more!

LEARN HOW TO:

- choose your words and actions wisely so you can tap into life's magic

- clear the energy in yourself and your environments for improved clarity, peace, and joy

- forgive, visualize, and trust in order to create a life of authenticity and abundance

- manifest lifelong health by improving nutrition, reducing stress, improving sleep, and more

- create your own unique angelic communication toolkit to help you to receive clear messages for yourself and others

- use the creative power of the quantum realm to create health and well-being

To find the guide for your journey,
visit www.HayHouseU.com.

HAY HOUSE
online learning

CONNECT WITH

HAY HOUSE
ONLINE

🌐 hayhouse.co.uk   **f** @hayhouse

📷 @hayhouseuk   𝕏 @hayhouseuk

▶ @hayhouseuk   ♪ @hayhouseuk

*Find out all about our latest books & card decks • Be the first
to know about exclusive discounts • Interact with our authors
in live broadcasts • Celebrate the cycle of the seasons with us
• Watch free videos from your favourite authors •
Connect with like-minded souls*

'*The gateways to wisdom and knowledge
are always open.*'

Louise Hay